ENDORSEMENTS

Mike and Andrea Brewer are a spiritual son and daughter who we have come to love and respect deeply. Sally and I have spent time with them in their home in Tennessee and have made several trips to their work in Haiti. What we have seen is both heart-warming and faith-building. The apostolic work they established there is the best example of a next-generation mission work we have witnessed anywhere in the world. Not only have they empowered the next generation to plant churches, they have successfully made their work indigenous, with Haitians leading the work long after the Brewers returned to the States.

Through their years in mission work Mike and Andrea have developed one of the best and most effective deliverance models we have ever encountered. Their new book *Bloodline Deliverance* takes the reader on their own personal journey into freedom. It is masterfully written, intensely personal, historically accurate, and theologically sound. This book is much more than theory; Mike and Andrea are effective practitioners who share testimonies of victories birthed in real-life encounters. A number of our friends and many members of our church family have found true freedom through their deliverance ministry. From our personal experience we can highly recommend their ministry and the life-changing principles you will find in this book.

Steve and Sally Wilson

Authors and Apostolic Leaders

Founding Pastors of Dayspring Church Springfield, Missouri

Apostolic Leadership team of International Connections

Apostolic Elders The Well Global Alliance

It is not every day I read a book on deliverance and spiritual warfare where I find it difficult to stop reading. However, this teaching had me gripped from topic to topic and page to page. I repeatedly found myself exclaiming out loud, "Wow! This is so good!" *Bloodline Deliverance* is a must-read for every leader, believer, and all who are engaged in deliverance ministry. You will be empowered with solid, in-depth, scriptural teaching along with revelation and the wisdom to walk out the truths revealed. Thank you, Michael and Andrea, for such an excellent teaching anointed with His presence, His truth, His Word, and the wisdom and authority from years of experience. It is my prayer this teaching and book will impact nations and many will be delivered into their Kingdom of Heaven inheritance of victorious redemption and freedom bringing glory to our Heavenly Father, Jesus, and Holy Spirit.

Rebecca Greenwood
Co-founder of Christian Harvest international
Strategic Apostolic Prayer Network
International Freedom Group
Christian Harvest Training Center

Early church fathers like Athanasius argued that one of the significant signs of the resurrection of Jesus is that demons are expelled. The same demons that obeyed Jesus as He walked the earth in a body still obey Jesus as He continues to move through His body, the Ekklesia.

I believe we are living in a time when there is a call back to the ancient path of discipleship, and part of the core value of discipleship is deliverance. Scholar Clinton Arnold argued that the four major components of discipleship of new converts in the early church included exorcism. Mike and Andrea do not just present an argument for bloodline deliverance; they invite us into the story of Jesus, the deliverer, setting His people free.

This book frames years of experience within a theological lens that I believe is part of a reformation of the signs that point to the victory of the Lamb King. I have been an eyewitness of the fruit of their ministry, so you have within your hands a treasure for generations to come.

Dr. Wayland Henderson
Founder of The Gathering Kingdom Center
Arlington, Texas

As in the days of old, my friends Mike and Andrea Brewer have stood firm in the ancient paths to recover a spiritual worldview of the Gospel. Their resource, *Bloodline Deliverance*, serves as a Kingdom manifesto urging the church to rise from complacency and engage in the battle for territory.

In a time when many skeptics ask, "Where is the promise of His coming?" Mike and Andrea guide us back to the gates of hell, reminding us of the apostolic truths and the victory delivered to us in the name of Jesus Christ. We are in a moment when the Lord is once again calling forth those who will recognize that He is the aggressor, leading us into a frontline Kingdom assault.

For all those eager to reach the front lines, this book is for you. It holds the keys to freedom for families, regions, and nations that are learning the power of becoming first-generation curse breakers. Just as the disciples of old discovered the power in the name of Christ, this book will open the eyes of many to see that demonic forces are still subject to His name.

May a new generation gain a front-row perspective that Satan has fallen and his kingdom is defeated.

Thank you, Mike and Andrea, for reminding us: "I have given you authority to trample on snakes and serpents and to overcome all the power of the enemy; nothing will harm you."

Tom Ledbetter
Founder of Kingdom Gravity Ministries Intl.
and The School of Dream Intelligence
Executive Director of Intelligence Solutions

I was in the middle of the most difficult season of ministry, both personally and publicly, when I began to cry out to God for answers as to why the enemy seemed to have so many legal rights to inflict me and those I loved with sickness, chaos, and destruction. In that dark night of the soul, fearing that I literally wouldn't survive the intense mental, physical, and emotional battle, I found myself stuck, then the word of the Lord came to me, saying, "The enemy has come to destroy you, but you, having done all to stand, stand therefore, and *I will deliver you.*"

At the time, I was perplexed by the Holy Spirit's statement, considering I was a prominent prophetic leader with an anointing specifically for healing trauma. I took extraordinary care of my soul as I submitted myself daily to the Lord's scrutiny. I was certain (so I thought) that I had already been delivered from any demons that I might have picked up through my rebellious years by simply renouncing all my sins and my ancestors' agreements with freemasonry. That was until, by divine providence, I was introduced to the bloodline deliverance method by Mike Brewer. As Jesus would have it, despite my condition contending for my own complete freedom, I got to know Mike while ministering alongside him on my first international missions trip to Australia.

I recall a man who came many miles to the meetings specifically to meet with Mike. The man had previously been thrown into a weeklong demonic trance when another minister had attempted deliverance on him. No one could get this young man free, no matter what they tried. With dark circles under his puffy, bloodshot eyes after weeks of torment, he sat across from Mike in a last-ditch and desperate effort for freedom. I stood in and watched firsthand the power, authority, and love of Christ coupled with the wisdom and knowledge that can only be obtained through years of experience flowing from Mike as he ministered to that young man's fractured soul, breaking curses and driving demons out of him. The man left the meeting totally free, hugging me and weeping with gratitude. Not long after that, Jesus, who is faithful to keep his promises, *delivered me* through my own personal deliverance session led by Mike. That was when I learned that unless a curse is actively broken and an identifiable demon is actively and effectively forced out, it will remain and continue to kill, steal, and destroy.

That trip changed the trajectory of my life and ministry. I have had the profound honor of building a relationship with Mike and Andrea. Their love, influence, and mentorship have been revolutionary, not just for myself but also for my family, my ministry team, my mentoring community and all their families—all of which have received bloodline deliverance training and ministry to some degree. Not only are we seeing tremendous breakthrough where there were only hindrances, but we have freedom from thoughts and emotions that we just thought were us! The purity, transparency, and peace in our homes, our relationships, and our meetings are tangible and profound.

Reader, what you hold in your hand is not only the most comprehensive, biblically sound, and historically accurate piece of literature on the topic of deliverance, but it is also a diabolical weapon of mass destruction to the powers of darkness. You hold in your hands the keys to set yourself, your family, and your city free from captivity. You hold in your hands the hope for future generations who will have the opportunity to live in peace tomorrow because you said "yes" to being trained for spiritual warfare today. If you are sick of watching the world around you suffer or are tired of settling for having less than the abundant life Christ died to give you, then it's time to join the fight. So pull the trigger, detonate this bomb of deliverance, and let's destroy hell.

Christa Elisha
Servant Founder of Arise Kingdom Ministries

There are times when certain people in a generation become important mile markers, helping the body of Christ recognize that a significant shift is available—one that leads to restoration and the fullness of times ahead. This is a new horizon, more than just the typical "new season" that many prophetic utterances reference. A mile marker stands, often weathered by the elements, yet maintaining the form intended by its manufacturer. It stands because it was built to stand, serving as a beacon of hope and a reminder of the true cost of the journey ahead.

Mike and Andrea represent an important mile marker in our generation—fashioned and formed to be tried and tested—so that many can find both hope and the cost in their own lives and leadership. Hope, because of what is available in, through, and with them; and cost, because of what is required of those who seek to tap into the treasure of these messengers and their message.

The messengers are to be trusted, and the message they carry in this book is to be approached with great care. When I first received a call about the deliverance occurring as described within these pages, I was skeptical—actually, very skeptical. Having been involved in and leading deliverance ministry for decades, I had seen countless exaggerations in how this kind of strategy was administered. This made me approach with caution. I did not seek proximity to the message; instead, the Lord first brought me into close proximity to the messengers. What I saw amazed me.

Mike and Andrea, rather than exuding great power and authority (which they have been given), primarily led with love. Every authentic expression of deliverance ministry must primarily be a ministry of love—love because God desires that one to be free, and love because everything standing between that one and their destiny is an enemy of the One who paid the ultimate price for them. Mike and Andrea lead deliverance like Jesus, often sacrificing greatly to serve the destiny of the one God places before them.

It was actually months after meeting them before I witnessed a bloodline deliverance, and not long after that, I found myself sitting in my own session, receiving a level of freedom that 23 years of deliverance ministry had missed. Yes, I needed it.

From that moment two and a half years ago until now, I have experienced and now lead bloodline deliverances, incorporating the principles, processes, and protocols described in these pages. I have done so in the same way I saw Mike and Andrea do it—with an expression of love. Not only are the concepts theologically sound, but the way in which the message is communicated does not grant permission for pride; rather, it calls for deeper submission to Jesus as the ultimate bloodline deliverer.

As we stand on the precipice of the greatest soul harvest our world has ever seen, and as time grows short for the readiness of those being thrust into the fields, the message of bloodline deliverance is a primary message to our generation. The Finisher is on the scene. The things that have lingered, been tolerated, and drawn children into tendencies and patterns that rob them of their rightful inheritance will no longer remain hidden deep within the bloodline. The Finisher is here, and generational curses are being exposed.

This book and the additional training Mike and Andrea provide make up a field manual for some of the most important finishers in our generation's history! Read this book, but don't stop there. Boldly and lovingly step into the pages within and your place in history.

Joshua Todd
Founder, East Gate Kingdom Fellowship

BLOODLINE DELIVERANCE

BLOODLINE DELIVERANCE

HOW TO SET YOURSELF, YOUR FAMILY, AND YOUR BLOODLINE FREE FROM DEMONS AND CURSES

MIKE & ANDREA BREWER

DESTINY IMAGE® PUBLISHERS, INC.
P.O. Box 310, Shippensburg, PA 17257-0310
"Publishing cutting-edge prophetic resources to supernaturally empower the body of Christ"

This book and all other Destiny Image and Destiny Image Fiction books are available at Christian bookstores and distributors worldwide.

For more information on foreign distributors, call 717-532-3040.
Reach us on the Internet: www.destinyimage.com.

ISBN 13 TP: 979-8-8815-0343-7
ISBN 13 eBook: 979-8-8815-0344-4
ISBN 13 Hardcover: 979-8-8815-0346-8
ISBN 13 Large Print: 979-8-8815-0347-5

For Worldwide Distribution, Printed in the U.S.A.
1 2 3 4 5 6 7 8 / 29 28 27 26 25

CONTENTS

INTRODUCTION

We are excited to share with you the wisdom, process, and testimonies that have come forth from *Bloodline Deliverance* in our many years of experience. One unique part of this book is that we wrote it together. In Chapter 1, you will have the opportunity to read Mike's story and how he first began in deliverance ministry over 26 years ago in a restaurant parking lot. From there, you will hear from both of us as we intertwine our writings among each section.

You will also notice different perspectives and writing styles between Mike and Andrea. Mike carries the gift of an apostle with much wisdom, insight, and experience, especially in deliverance ministry. He writes through this perspective and shares lots of stories and testimonies throughout this book, which is built upon his over 26 years of experience and ministry.

Andrea carries the gifts of a prophet and a teacher. For the last ten years, she has lived in the realm of the academic world as she finished her bachelor's degree from Family of Faith Christian University (FFCU) and then completed her master's degree in Biblical Studies through Global Awakening Theological Seminary (GATS). She currently teaches courses online at the bachelor's level for Family of Faith Christian University. As a result, she carries a more formal and scholarly writing style utilizing endnotes and thorough research. Her heart is to provide the theological foundation through the Bible as well as context, through history and research, for the experiences that we encounter frequently in *Bloodline Deliverance.* If you are unfamiliar with endnotes, these are simply the research behind her writing and also a place for you to find additional information on a specific topic.

Concerning the stories shared in this book, each one is true and from our own personal experiences; these are not fictional nor are they metaphors or just fictional examples. We have changed names and left out certain details in order to ensure anonymity and protect those who have been through horrible life experiences from demonization. It is also important to note that all of the commentaries that were used are published within the last 25 years to ensure the most accurate and recent research available.

This book was truly written by us, together. Let's dive in!

Mike and Andrea

CHAPTER 1

VICTORY ON VOODOO MOUNTAIN

MIKE'S STORY

My heart was beating out of my chest as my team and I descended deep inside the voodoo caves. We were all very aware that death could be waiting for us as we obeyed Jesus's command to take the Gospel to every creature according to Mark 16:15. One year before our arrival, we learned of the wickedness that was taking place in this region of Haiti. The news of possible human sacrifice provoked us to take action.

One of our principal keys in church-planting is to find the darkest places and take the Gospel to these locations as a demonstration that Jesus was actually victorious over all things. As we began to pray into the strategy, we contacted one of our apostolic team leaders and asked him to go scout the land and discover if God had prepared a person of peace to receive us.[1] His testimony was shared with us:

> As I prayed about going to the area, an angel came and stood before me. The angel showed me a picture of a man named Ernesto. The angel said, "Go and find Ernesto." As I arrived in the territory of 40,000 people, I began to

> inquire of anyone named Ernesto. After several days, I discovered two people, but they were not the one the angel had revealed to me. I arrived at the last person's home, and the daughter of Ernesto told me her father, the third Ernesto, would be home soon. I sat outside waiting for his arrival. Finally, I saw him walking down the dirt road. I declared to him with excitement, "You are the man the angel told me to find! He said that you would receive us in the territory." Immediately, in fear, Ernesto fell to his knees declaring, "This cannot be me as I am only a lukewarm Christian!"

Ernesto repented and returned to the Lord that day. He also connected our leader to several others in the body of Christ, which opened the door for our ministry to begin working in the area.

Over the weeks ahead, my team and I visited the area and conducted a small meeting with local Christian leaders, pastors, teachers, and evangelists in the area. I remember the day of this particular training. I stood in front of men and women who loved God and had held on to what little ground the Gospel had taken, but they were beat up and spiritually weak by the continual onslaught of demonic attacks. I began to encourage them and thank them for their faithfulness to Christ and to each other. I further shared with them that our gift to the body of Christ was of the apostolic and prophetic nature. God was using us to bring forth vision and strategy to the local, existing churches there because He wanted this territory for His name.

It was a great day when they received us with humility. Over the next days, we trained them in the supernatural and in church-planting from house to house. We also shared how it was our desire to return in one year and conduct a small crusade in direct confrontation of the town's annual, seven-day voodoo ceremony. Voodoo priests and practitioners would come from all over the world to participate in this wicked festival. Voodoo is the predominant religion of Haiti, which is a mixture of African animistic worship and Catholicism; it is very demonic. These local leaders were elated with this plan!

During these initial meetings, there was an 86-year-old pastor whom we will call Joel. Pastor Joel began to share about voodoo mountain, a place that had been given over to darkness. This mountain contained a large cave system that went down several hundred feet before finally opening up to what we called the ceremonial room. This was the place where they offered animal, and some even said human, sacrifices to the evil spirits of voodoo. As Joel continued to share with us, I could feel his broken heart over the people who were in terrible fear and bondage to the dark demons that were worshiped in his homeland. "In my lifetime," declared Pastor Joel, "the Gospel has never been preached on this mountain."

Those words penetrated my heart. This man of God, as wonderful as he was, had tolerated this darkness towering over both his life and also the lives of the hundreds of families in that area. What was "normal" for Pastor Joel was actually not normal nor acceptable. The Gospel demands confrontation with these evil powers. This led us into a strategy: to carry the Gospel covertly for the next year from house to house and establish new house churches in connection with the more traditional churches of the region. Thirty-three new churches were birthed over that next year! Great hope and faith began to fill the people of God as they assembled and began carrying intercession for their homeland.

Finally, the time had arrived for me and a small team to lead a crusade in the middle of the city and proclaim Jesus inside the voodoo caves on the mountain! The town was filled with a multitude of practitioners of voodoo from Haiti and even other nations. You could feel the tension in the air and warfare in the spirit as we proclaimed the Gospel of Jesus and called people to repentance. I stood in front of nearly 4,500 people and taught them on personal, family, village, regional, and national levels of deliverance. That night, many people received Jesus as Savior and Lord, repenting of their sins, turning away from voodoo, and turning to Christ.

The next morning was the day of ascending voodoo mountain for the purpose of preaching the Gospel to all who were inside the caves and offering sacrifices to demons. I was reminded of Paul, Elijah, Gideon, and others who had walked into wicked places and risked their lives because they loved Jesus and people. As we got closer to the mouth of the cave, we could hear the sounds of drums and demon worship coming from the ceremonial room deep inside the cave. With sweat pouring down my face, my heart was pounding with the realization that my team and I might be martyred for the sake of the Gospel. After a year of fasting, preparing, and planting churches across this remote region of Haiti, it all came down to this moment of confrontation.

Only hours before, I had met with my team and released them from any obligation of going into this voodoo cave to preach the Gospel. The sincerity of the moment was gripping as we were confronting our own personal fears and the intimidating demons behind the wicked voodoo system. Compelled by the love of

Jesus, we descended deeper into the cave system and approached the beating rhythms of the voodoo drums.

We finally entered the ceremonial room; it was cold, dark, and musty with only the light of candles and a few rays of sunshine coming through a hole in the top of the mountain. We could see a bloody cow that had just been sacrificed to these evil gods. Inside the room were approximately 25 people plus eight voodoo priests holding their knives, which they had just used to sacrifice the cow on the altar. My team and I began to share the Gospel. Being overtaken by the Holy Spirit, I jumped up on top of the bloody cow and began to proclaim the death, burial, and resurrection of Jesus. During this time, the voodoo priests lifted their hands while holding their daggers and backed up against the wall, as if in full surrender to the angelic hosts that were with us in that moment.

Conviction began to come upon those in the room as Jesus was exalted high above all other rulers and powers. Two ladies looked up at me, and through the beautiful Creole language said, "We received Jesus today." They stood to their feet and started removing what they called their "devil clothing." This was a part of voodoo rituals with different colored garments representing different demons that they worshiped. It was a beautiful sight to see as they came to know Jesus as their Lord and Savior in that very moment! As the Gospel went forth in demonstrative power, many evil "gods" were confronted, and the power of sin was broken! Everyone in the cave system came to know Jesus that day!

After several hours in the cave, sharing the Gospel and witnessing great victory, these new believers joined my team and began to sing "Victory in Jesus" in Creole as we marched out of the cave system. I was walking behind the group of nearly sixty people, and by the time I exited the caves, the former voodoo practitioners had built a fire outside and were burning all of the items they used to worship the false demon gods. What a beautiful sight to behold! Transformation had begun, but it would not stop here.

Later that evening, we were at the crusade in the middle of the city. As these testimonies were going forth, there was a woman who began shouting in the middle of the crowd of over 4,500 people. Many of the leaders ran out and brought her to me. After some investigation, we learned that she had been blind for over ten years, and she was shouting, "I can see! I can see!" Everyone from the town knew who she was and that she was blind. Now, she could see!

The apostolic leader, whom we had sent to the town a year prior, took to the stage and began to declare this was a sign and a miracle from God that He was removing decades of darkness from the region and causing their God-given sight to return! A blanket of darkness and deception was removed from this region during this great deliverance! God is always faithful to show up when we step out in faith. The light of Christ has the power to penetrate even the darkest places of the earth and release the power of the Gospel to heal, deliver, and save!

CALLED BY GOD

It was 2:30 AM, nearly 26 years ago, as I lay in my bed praying because I was unable to sleep from working the night shift at a local factory. While praying, I was taken up into a vision. I heard the Lord speak into my right ear, "I am calling you!" Those words were terrifying to me as I was not a speaker. To be honest, I had cheated my way through high school and took zeroes on all public speaking assignments because I refused to do them.

With this fear gripping my heart, I rolled out of bed onto my knees and began to pour my heart out to Jesus. As I was confessing these fears, I was also committing to follow what He had just said to me. I was overtaken by the Holy Spirit in that moment. Soon after, I was on my back with deep groans coming from deep within my spirit. The groans continued for over half an hour. With each one, my body would curl up like doing a sit-up or crunches. Once this moment began to cease, I returned to my knees not knowing or understanding what had just happened within me.

Growing up, my mom would take me to the local, traditional Pentecostal church, and I would hear and see people praying in another language called tongues. However, this experience was definitely not that; it was different. Had I prayed in tongues that night, I would have been okay with it. Since this was distinctively different, I was concerned that I had just experienced something outside of the biblical framework. Therefore, I began to ask God to show me in His Word what had just happened within me. I heard the Holy Spirit speak to me so clearly that morning: "Get up, go downstairs, get your Bible, and turn to John chapter 11, verse 33." I was shocked to have heard Him so clearly, but I followed those words immediately.

This passage says, "*When Jesus saw her weeping, and the Jews who had come along with her also weeping, he was deeply moved in spirit and troubled*" (John 11:33 NIV). It describes when Jesus was going to the tomb of Lazarus and was met by Mary. As she told Him that He was too late, Jesus groaned within Himself. At that time, I could finally explain what that groaning actually was and that it was biblical. This set my heart at ease, and I began to grow rapidly in my walk with the Lord after this encounter.

A DEMON LEFT ME

Shortly after this encounter and my calling from the Lord, I began to fast and pray. My fasting and prayer was for God to deliver me from a pornography addiction that I had since I was 12 years old. At that time, a police officer in my hometown gave me a bag of pornographic magazines. Yes, porn magazines! Although I was no longer actively looking at porn, I could not get those images, thoughts, and compulsions out of my mind. My fast was motivated by a deeper repentance and a desire to be free from these images.

While I was nearing the third day of a water-only fast, I was standing in a church during the Sunday evening service when a man I didn't know came up and put his arm around my shoulders. He laid his hand on my chest and said, "Father, forgive him as this has become an addiction." At that moment, there was a tangible explosion that burst out of my chest, and I fell limp onto the floor. I will never forget that moment as long as I live. The purity and righteousness of God were moving through me in waves. My mind was clear for the first time since I was 12 years old and first looked at those magazines. As I lay on the floor, deep sobs of joy and love for Jesus filled me. I can tell you that without question, a demon left me that day! I do not know the name of that particular demon, but it was gone and my life produced the fruits of that deliverance.

MY FIRST FORTY-DAY FAST

Although I had no formal training or mentorship during this season, my deliverance led to a deeper desire to grow in the Lord and preach His Word. Over the next few weeks, I was asked to go on my first international missions trip to the country of Panama. Shortly after, while visiting a small rural Baptist church, I was asked to preach my first message. These two opportunities lead to an urgency for accelerated growth. Since my last request came during a fast, I began another fast, but this was a partial fast of eating one meal per day for the next forty days.

These were beautiful days of reading the New Testament all the way through several times and growing in intimacy with Jesus. At the end of the fast, I preached my first message through fear and terror. Actually, it was not theologically sound at all, but the church gave me grace and celebrated my desire to serve God. Once that assignment was complete, I got on a plane with a small mission team and took off to Panama. It is important to understand that I was a mountain boy and rarely ever left the mountains of East Tennessee; going to another country was a massive endeavor.

As the plane approached the landing strip in Panama, my heart was beating fast, and I had no idea what the next seven days would hold. I remember getting out of the seat with my backpack and walking down the portable stairway onto the tarmac. As soon as my feet touched the ground, I again heard the Holy Spirit say, "You are stepping into an apostolic office." My first thought was, *Well, what is that?* I had no grid or understanding as to what this could mean, and I certainly was not going to ask anyone because most of the people around me did not understand that God was still speaking to His people. It would be 18 years later before I was recognized and commissioned as an apostle in the body of Christ.

A DANGEROUS PRAYER

As I continued in my growth in scripture and my relationship with Jesus, He was opening my eyes at a rapid pace in comparison to my peers who seemed to love God but were not burning for His presence like I was. I remember one significant day in which I was sitting on the couch in my house, reading my Bible and praying, when I came across a familiar passage in the book of Matthew. This is the chapter where Jesus calls His disciples together and gives them authority to drive out demons and to heal all sickness and disease:

> *As you go, proclaim this message: "The kingdom of heaven has come near." Heal the sick, raise the dead, cleanse those who have leprosy, drive out demons. Freely you have received; freely give* (Matthew 10:7-8 NIV).

As I read this scripture, it was as if it jumped off the pages and came into my heart. The response came out of me through the following prayer: "God, I don't see a lot of people casting out demons today, so feel free to use me in that manner." Little did I know that the prayer I prayed that day would thrust me into a battle that I was ill-equipped to handle at that time.

EXORCISM DEFEAT AT A PUBLIC RESTAURANT

About a week after praying this prayer, I was sitting at an Applebee's restaurant late one evening that was about to close for the night. Everyone had left already from our group except for me and one other friend. His son had just left to go to their truck, leaving the two of us sitting there. It felt odd, like something was about to happen. The man turned to me and said, "I've been waiting for them to leave. Mike, why can't I be free like other people?"

Now, I would not call this man a close friend but more of an acquaintance. I knew his name, but not much else at the time. He was a relatively new believer, and when he asked me this question, something in the atmosphere shifted. Even though I could not have told you what a word of knowledge was at this time, the Holy Spirit dropped one in my spirit. I found myself responding to him, "Maybe there is a point of pain in your life that hasn't been healed yet."

The moment I said "point of pain," his face contorted into something that I will never forget. It was as if pure evil was staring back at me through his eyes, and his expression snarled in a way that still haunts me to this day, over twenty-five years later. I had just prayed the previous week, "God, if You want to use me in this area, I'm ready." I was a young believer, full of energy, and fired up with passion and zeal. Now, just a week later, here was the very answer to that prayer staring me straight in the face. I was ready—or at least, I thought I was.

I stood up and said, "Brother, let's go outside. I want to pray for you." We walked to the back of my truck. It was almost closing time for the restaurant now. I put my arm around him, laid my hand on his shoulder, and said, "In the name of Jesus, I confront you." What happened next startled me. He let out a growl—"Rah!"—and collapsed to the ground. I was shocked. I had read about this kind of thing and seen people fall out in church, but nothing like this and to this extreme.

At this time, I was in good physical shape, practicing jiu-jitsu, and I thought to myself, *I need to hold him down. What if he tries to run out onto the highway and hurt himself?* So I dropped down with my knee on his belly and commanded, "In the name of Jesus, who are you?" His face contorted in a way I had never seen before. Through his gritted teeth, he sneered, "I am Lust." Today, I would have known to call out the higher demonic authority, but back then, I was taken aback. This was my first encounter with something like this. Inside, I was shaking. I tried to keep my composure, but all I could think internally was, *If the police show up, I am going to jail for assault!*

As the wrestle continued, I thought I would try again, "Come out of him, Lust," but the demon laughed at me and mocked me all the more. I felt like all the faith I had inside just left me in that instant. I was using the name of Jesus; how could this demon be mocking me, and not just mocking me, but using a feminine tone of voice? I knew how to say the words, but I did not yet know how to enforce the authority behind them.

Fear crept in. I remembered the story of the Jewish exorcists in the Bible, the ones who were overpowered and stripped naked by the demons they tried to cast out.[2] Was that going to happen to me now? Then, the man's face began to return to normal, and he looked at me after a few minutes, finally able to speak. He asked, "Mike, what's going on?" I was glad the demon was down, but my heart was still racing as I knew this was not over. I told him, "You've got some spiritual issues, and I'm calling our pastor." I did not want to be alone with this guy any longer. I called my pastor, and he told me to meet him at someone's house to deal with the situation.

When we arrived, it was just the three of us—two men who had read a few books about deliverance and a pastor, all trying to deal with this demon. We wrestled with that spirit and fought with it until after 3:30 AM. This man finally shared with us that his uncle had raped him. Once we led him through forgiveness for his uncle, it seemed that the demon was gone, or at least, we hoped it was gone. By the time we finished, we all prayed that it was actually gone. In that moment though, I realized just how unprepared I was.

A few days later, my pastor came to me and said, "Mike, you need to start teaching deliverance classes." I thought to myself, *Oh Lord, no! I'm not ready for that.* I could barely wrap my head around what had just happened, let alone teach others what to do. I told him, "Pastor, I don't know how to do this." He looked at me and said, "Well, right now, you're the second most-experienced person we've got in the church." I could not believe it. Internally, I thought, *Wow, Jesus. Other than the pastor, if I'm the most experienced we've got, then we are in serious trouble.* We had just opened up a huge spiritual battle, and I was not sure how to fight it. Somehow, very reluctantly, I agreed to start the classes.

At that time, we were having services in a large crusade tent with a double-wide trailer set up behind it. During our midweek service, we announced the launch of the deliverance class. Guess who the first person to show up was? Yes, my buddy from the restaurant—the same guy who I had just had that intense encounter with several days before. By this point, I had read a little more from a book on deliverance, but it had only been about two weeks since that night in the restaurant parking lot. I was thrown right into the deep end, but sometimes, this is the life when God has us on an accelerated path.

The following week, my first deliverance class started. There were about eight people in the room, and my buddy came in looking troubled. He said to me, "Mike, I'm hearing voices."

To be honest, I was not surprised. Then, he said something that caused a deep, righteous anger to rise up in me: "Now, I'm hearing suicidal voices." I was angry, not at him but at the enemy. He had experienced a touch of God's power, even if he was not fully delivered yet. He knew God was real and that the Lord was working in his life, but now, this spirit was tormenting him again and pushing him harder toward something as dark as suicide. I just could not tolerate this.

I turned around and commanded, "Demon, get to attention!" Instantly, the demon manifested again with a deep growl. "Rah!" I asked it, "Who are you?" and the same answer came back: "I am Lust." I was frustrated and responded, "I told you to leave last time. Why didn't you go?" The demon replied, "The curse." The curse? This caught my attention. "What curse?" I demanded to know. The spirit answered back, "Incest." During our previous session, my friend had confessed that he had been sexually abused, but he had said it was by his uncle. So I pressed further, asking, "Incest from whom?" And the demon answered, "His father."

I was stunned. My friend had admitted that his uncle had abused him but not his dad. It was clear now that he had been carrying deep shame while trying to protect his father's reputation. We all knew his dad, and I could see that the shame had kept him in bondage. It was not just the physical abuse, but it was the emotional and spiritual heaviness of trying to protect his dad, even at his own expense. I bound the demon and brought my friend back to awareness.

"Hey man," I said. "You told us that it was your uncle who abused you, not your dad. What's going on?" He looked at me, wide-eyed, and asked, "How did you know?" I told him, "The Lord made that demon tell me." We both knew what had to be done. I said, "You need to forgive your dad. Let's break this curse off of you and off of your family." And when he renounced the sin and forgave his father, the spirit of Lust finally left him. There was no more laughing and no more mocking, just a moment of release and of freedom.

It is amazing how a small amount of truth and understanding can unlock someone's freedom. What had held him captive for years was suddenly gone in the name of Jesus, and I saw, firsthand, the power of forgiveness and breaking curses. This was a powerful lesson that I would never forget.

LOVE OR POWER ENCOUNTER

After my first demon encounter at an Applebee's restaurant and the pastor subsequently asking me to start leading deliverance classes, I spent two years conducting weekly deliverance sessions at that local church. Those two years were a time of immense learning and growth as I discovered how to persevere, love, and empower others toward freedom. However, near the end of that period, I had a profound encounter with Jesus. He spoke to me and said, "Mike, you love the power encounter more than you love My people." Over 20 years later, those words still weigh heavily on my heart. They were absolutely true, though I had not realized it until Jesus revealed it to me. Before being called by God and walking with Him, I was a mixed-martial artist who trained in jiu-jitsu and MMA-style fighting. After Jesus spoke to me, I recognized that my approach to deliverance carried the same adrenaline rush that I had experienced while fighting.

As I reflected on His words, brokenness arose from within me. I knew I had to ask Him to teach me how to love others and to give me a compassionate heart for His people. That moment marked a turning point in my ministry and my life. After hearing those words and reflecting on them, deliverances almost completely ceased for the next several years because I had to learn to love first. I loved the power encounter more than the person in front of me. Love had to be developed within me, as deliverance had become more about how it made me feel, what I could do for Jesus, and the testimonies that would follow rather than about genuine love and compassion for the person being delivered.

As Jesus taught me to love, deliverance returned to our ministry and our lives. Today, I never begin a deliverance session or even preach at a church without first praying: "Father, give me Your heart and Your love for the people I will minister to today." I do not move forward until I feel His presence and love for those people. I've come to understand the truth of Scripture: "Faith works through love."[3]

This lesson became especially clear during a challenging New Year's Eve situation involving a survivor of satanic ritual abuse (SRA). This person had arrived at the church hours before our New Year's Eve celebration, and we had planned to do some deliverance ministry with her. Just minutes before midnight, a programmed part of her psyche manifested. This part was deeply controlled by demonic forces whose sole purpose was to drive her back to a ritual site for a New Year's ceremony every year. This part of her was so demonized and under such control of evil spirits that my team and I could not break its hold during the session. In desperation, we brought her back to our home, where she stayed with my wife and me for three days. Yes, that's correct—for three full days, we fought against the demonic powers that were controlling her. It took that long to break their influence.

While I will not delve into all the depths of that story here, I share this to emphasize that deliverance ministry is a ministry of great love and compassion. It can only be sustained through the supernatural love of Jesus; to love as He loved is the ultimate goal. It is a simple truth with a profoundly supernatural application. My prayer for you is that as you continue in this journey, you will learn to love well as Jesus exemplified. Deliverance ministry is not just about confronting the demonic; it is also about carrying the heart of Jesus for the people He loves so dearly.

CHAPTER 2

JESUS CONFRONTS THE FALSE GOD OF DEATH

The power of direct confrontation and authoritative commands is a crucial key to setting the captives free. When confronting demons, clarity and specificity in commands are essential. Vague prayers or general commands will not suffice. For example, prayers like, "God, will You set this person free?" are irrelevant and will not bring deliverance. Instead, we must speak directly to the demon with clear, authoritative commands such as, "Come out," "Obey," "Be quiet," and similar directives.

> *Now when Jesus came into the district of Caesarea Philippi, he asked his disciples, "Who do people say that the Son of Man is?" And they said, "Some say John the Baptist but others Elijah and still others Jeremiah or one of the prophets." He said to them, "But who do you say that I am?" Simon Peter answered, "You are the Messiah, the Son of the living God." And Jesus answered him, "Blessed are you, Simon son of Jonah! For flesh and blood has not revealed this to you but my Father in heaven. And I tell you, you are Peter, and on this rock* ***I will build my church, and the gates of Hades will not prevail against it.*** *I will give you the keys of the*

kingdom of heaven, and whatever you bind on earth will be bound in heaven, and whatever you loose on earth will be loosed in heaven" (Matthew 16:13-19 NRSV).

This is the famous passage where Jesus reveals His church. He could have chosen any place for this revelation, so why did He choose Caesarea Philippi? What was unique about this place?

The reference to the rock was a physical location that Jesus was standing on at that moment located at Caesarea Philippi, at the foot of Mount Hermon.[4] In the Old Testament, this same location served as an idolatrous worship hub under King Jeroboam[5] as well as a Canaanite worship center for Baal.[6] In the early first century, this same location was also called "Panias" as it served as the worship center for the demonic deity of Pan.[7] The cult of Pan was central to Caesarea Philippi, and a large cave at the base of Mount Hermon, fed by a spring, was considered a sacred cave dedicated to this demon and other false gods.

Near this cave was the most famous shrine to Pan, which locals believed to be the gateway to the underworld in which it is presumed that Hades was the gatekeeper. The Temple of Zeus, who was known as the brother of Hades, was located near the cave of Pan. Zeus was the chief god in the Greek pantheon, and his worship in Caesarea Philippi was another indication of the city's central place in the pagan religious world. Jesus, as well as those present for this encounter, would have been familiar with both the past and current contexts of this location as well as the understanding that it had been a sacrificial worship center for many demonic deities for thousands of years. The supernatural understanding of this location cannot be quickly dismissed or overlooked.

It was here that rituals and sacrifices took place, including animal sacrifices thrown into the cave waters. The King James Version famously translates verse 18 to say, "*The gates of hell shall not prevail against it.*" Much of the modern church has widely accepted this translation by implying that "hell," as a place of eternal torment or damnation, will not be able to stand against the church and her salvation in Jesus. Some have placed this passage within a message that every power of hell can wage war against the church without limits, but as long as believers just "hold on" until Jesus returns, they will eventually be saved. This interpretation alludes to a powerless church just barely existing and struggling to win the cosmic war between the demonic realm and the earthly realm. It also implies that the church is only on the defensive side of this cosmic battle, just waiting for enemy attacks, and not progressing forward in an offensive posture. A further problem with this translation is that the word "hell" is not actually used, but instead, the proper name, "Hades."

JESUS'S DECLARATION OF WAR

It is significant that Jesus chose to visit this location. This area, known for its idolatry and deep-rooted paganism, was not typical of Jewish towns where Jesus normally preached. It was in this spiritual atmosphere of false gods, emperor worship, and demonic influences that Jesus made His declaration of the establishment of the church. The city was symbolic of the world Jesus was coming to reclaim—a world filled with darkness, demon worship, and demonic control. His decision to go to Caesarea Philippi and declare His Messiahship in this very spot was a declaration of war against the demonic deities. Imagine

Jesus pointing at the high-level demonic gods and goddesses and declaring, "I will build My church, and the gates of Hades will not prevail against it!"

This is a direct, confrontational statement with the ruling false gods of the territory. Jesus's disciples would have known He was being extremely confrontational with such a profound statement. It was a challenge, authoritative and highly provocative. In the spirit, it was an act of war.

JESUS'S EXAMPLE OF AUTHORITY

There is a profound lesson in Jesus deliberately entering a dark place and addressing Hades by name. This was neither passive nor coincidental. By choosing such a setting and confronting one of the region's ruling principalities, He was demonstrating His authority and instilling confidence in His disciples about who He truly was as the Son of God.

On another occasion, Jesus sent His disciples out, granting them power over unclean spirits to cast them out.[8] In doing so, they actively participated in dismantling territorial, demonic strongholds, following the example He had set for them. Therefore, every act of deliverance fits within the larger framework of Jesus reclaiming territory back from these ruling powers and thus establishing His Kingdom.

DEMONIC SHOWDOWNS: SHAKING REGIONS

Throughout my years of church-planting in Haiti and India, I have learned several key principles when entering a new territory. One of these principles is to always ask God for a breakthrough miracle or deliverance. These moments are crucial as they show people in the region that Jesus is King, Lord, and Master over all. Oftentimes, people in nations like Haiti or India live in fear from the false, religious gods of their culture. They are ensnared by schemes that are designed to silence them and prevent them from confronting the territorial spirits.

Recently, I traveled to India to lead a training for about 500 Christian leaders on how to conduct deliverance. Upon my arrival, I noticed that many of these leaders were deeply fearful about what might happen at the conference. As we discussed the nation's various gods, they were reluctant to even say the names of these deities out loud, fearing retribution or punishment. This fear was so ingrained that they asked me to remove specific references from the books that I had planned to distribute in their local language. However, I refused and explained that what they had tolerated until now must be confronted for the sake of setting the people free.

As the conference began, I taught on the foundational process of bloodline deliverance. During the curse-breaking portion of the session, a man seated midway back in the church stood up and began a demonic dance and chanted wildly. I recognized this as the breakthrough moment I had been praying for, specifically asking God for one of the Hindu demonic trinity—Brahma, Vishnu, or Shiva—to manifest. These deities form what I call the "Demonic Trinity" of Hinduism, and everyone in attendance knew their significance. My prayer was that one of these spirits would manifest so that we could publicly demonstrate the authority of Jesus over them and set the church free from its fear.

As the young man continued to manifest, I asked some men to bring him forward. Addressing the attendees, I explained, "This is not how deliverance is typically done, but I'm demonstrating both the process of deliverance and Christ's authority over all evil spirits." I designated the audience as the prayer team while I led the deliverance. Turning to the demon, I commanded, "In Jesus's name, tell me your name!" The demon reacted violently and threatened to kill me and everyone else present. I persisted and demanded to know its name in Jesus's authority. After several minutes of resistance, the demon finally cried out, "My name is Trimurti." I was initially disappointed because I had hoped for Brahma, Vishnu, or Shiva.

As the deliverance continued, we identified and broke the legal rights the demon had over the young man. Once those rights were nullified, we began casting out the demon. However, it was powerful and stubborn and refused to leave. I commanded, "You will bow before the Lord Jesus, acknowledging His authority and power over you. When your knees touch the ground, you will come out of this man." I instructed the prayer team to join me in forcing the demon to bow in the name of Jesus. The entire process took about 45 minutes, but eventually, Trimurti knelt and left the young man, who was then set free. The fear that had gripped the Christian leaders broke as they witnessed this demonstration of Jesus's authority firsthand. Their faith was transformed into something experiential and unshakable.

I continued leading the group in curse-breaking prayers. As we prayed, hundreds of people began manifesting demons, with some literally crawling down the aisles like lions, tigers, and serpents. Yet, Jesus was faithful and set them free! For several hours, my team and I cast demons out of the leaders. By the end of this time, these leaders were emboldened as they had also been delivered from fear and were now empowered to cast out demons themselves.

As the conference concluded, I expressed disappointment that Brahma,Vishnu, or Shiva had not manifested for the demonstration. The leaders corrected me, explaining that Trimurti represented a trinitarian fusion of Brahma, Vishnu, and Shiva—a revelation that astounded me.This deliverance was a breakthrough for everyone present and further provided a powerful demonstration of Jesus's authority. It also aligned perfectly with Mark 1:28, which speaks of Jesus's fame spreading throughout the region.

This experience reaffirmed the importance of bringing deliverance into public spaces rather than relegating it to back rooms, offices, or counseling sessions. Public demonstrations of the Gospel's power over unclean spirits break fear and complacency and birth movements of great faith.When deliverance is hidden away, we miss opportunities to showcase the Gospel's transformative power.

A MANDATE OF INTERCESSION

After the Lord called Andrea and I back to our hometown of Maryville,Tennessee, we began planting an apostolic center called The Well of Maryville.We refused to rely on marketing programs or transfer growth from other churches. Instead, we committed to planting as the Lord brought people and would continue in intercession until He moved.

To share a pivotal moment, my wife joined Dr. Sam Matthews on a trip to Wales in 2019, visiting the Bible College of Wales where the ministry of Rees Howells had taken place. During her week of intercession for the nations, I stayed behind with our youngest daughter. One morning, we went to our church to pray, which was not unusual, but this time, I felt an urgency from the Lord. As I knelt at the altar, the Lord spoke clearly: "I am giving you a mandate of intercession for the full eradication of witchcraft and occult powers from the region." The weight of His words pressed heavily on my spirit.

Having planted churches in Haiti and India, I understood the gravity of the term *region* and recognized this as a serious, God-given mandate. It was something that could only be accomplished through persistent intercession in Christ. I shared this with our elders, and after much prayer, we all felt confident that this was from the Lord. Together, we began praying for this mandate to come to fruition, knowing that it would require perseverance and the labor of Christ through us to bring heaven's will to east Tennessee.

Deliverance had already been a consistent part of my ministry for the previous 26 years, both domestically and internationally. It was not an occasional occurrence but a foundational aspect of our work. Yet, the level of deliverance we were about to experience in response to this intercession was unlike anything I had ever encountered. Within weeks, demons began manifesting at unprecedented levels. Witches started attending our services; we faced opposition from people involved with the Masonic Lodge. One morning, I found a gutted bird on our church doorstep. Through intercession, spiritual strongholds that had never been touched in our region began to shake.

Initially, I led all the deliverances myself, but as the volume grew, I realized that this was unsustainable. I began training team members to lead deliverances and appointing leaders for each team. We were conducting multiple deliverances every week when, one day, during prayer, God spoke to us again: "It is time to go public." At first, I did not understand what that meant, but it became clear that He was directing us to take deliverance ministry into the public sphere. I shared this with our leadership team, and after confirmation, we all agreed that it was, again, the word of the Lord for us.

The following Sunday, I prayed for emotional healing during the service, and demons began to manifest. I brought one man forward and told the congregation, "Church, you have just been promoted to the intercessory prayer team fighting for this man's soul." As the deliverance unfolded, a visiting couple was touched by the Holy Spirit, fell to the floor, and began praying in tongues for the first time. This moment was a testament to the power of public deliverance ministry and its ability to awaken people to their need for the Holy Spirit. We realized firsthand that, "Deliverance brings the believer into a greater revelation of the power of the cross."[9]

Of course, public deliverance stirred criticism from religious observers who questioned its appropriateness. However, scripture reveals that most deliverances performed by Jesus occurred in public, and I believe the lack of public demonstrations of God's power contributes to the church's seeming impotence in many aspects. While some churches operate in the supernatural power of God, they often relegate such work to only backrooms or private sessions. Thus, they often miss the opportunity to showcase God's power and inspire others to take up their spiritual ministry.

Shortly after, we launched our first monthly, public deliverance night. Open to anyone in the region, these nights quickly became a demonstrative display of God's authority and power. During our inaugural meeting, as I led the congregation through curse-breaking declarations, demons began manifesting everywhere. Longtime Christians were rolling on the floor and screaming out loudly, but Christ was glorified, and people were set free. These monthly deliverance nights have continued for the last four years. Over the next two years, we multiplied deliverance teams and started holding sessions almost daily. In the past year alone, we have documented over 1,400 deliverances, expanded into online sessions and further, trained leaders all across the United States and beyond, even into other nations as well.

THE CHURCH FILLED WITH DEMONS

When this level of deliverance began at The Well, our local church, my fellow leaders and I were completely caught off guard. It was shocking to confront the extent of demonization within our congregation. While I don't have exact numbers, a significant percentage of our members were affected. These were not individuals from diverse religious backgrounds; most had been raised in professing Christian households. Of course, we know that simply professing Christianity does not necessarily make one a true believer or follower of Jesus. Still, what stood out was that our congregation was not composed of people coming out of witchcraft or overtly occult practices. These were ordinary, everyday believers.

Trust me when I say that this brought extreme tensions within the congregation. Many people simply did not want to deal with demonization; they just wanted to come to church, have a normal service, and go home. But as demons manifested publicly and required immediate attention, the situation called for great love and compassion from the leadership. We learned to love people even when we felt deeply uncomfortable with what we were witnessing. Yes, some people left the church and accused us of being too focused on demons and darkness. However, this was far from the truth. Our focus was on loving people enough to fight for their freedom and not giving up on them and the destiny Jesus had for their lives. We chose to prevail, more determined than ever to see the people of God set free.

I want to share a story about Sarah, a member of our congregation. She reached out to me concerning her debilitating social anxiety. The fear of interacting with others triggered extreme panic attacks, causing her to shut down both emotionally and physically. Her anxiety was so severe that she had to arrive late and leave early from church to avoid any form of social conversations. Some days, she could not make it to church at all and would turn around halfway through her commute due to being so overwhelmed by panic attacks.

Sarah's insecurities ran deep, robbed her of joy, and strained her relationships with her husband and her loved ones. Anxiety and fear were stealing her God-given ability to enjoy life. Having heard me speak about freedom and witnessing some of the deliverances taking place during services, she decided to confront the possibility that a demon might be influencing her. I remember our first meeting vividly: she came in literally trembling with fear. Not long after, the demon named Lilith manifested in her, which had entered through childhood sexual abuse. After casting out Lilith and several other demons, Sarah experienced incredible freedom. She no longer suffers from extreme anxiety attacks and can now fully participate in worship and all forms of social fellowship with friends and family.

Another powerful testimony comes from Rick, a good man in his mid-thirties who deeply loves God and his family. Rick had served in several churches and ministries and earned a strong reputation in both ministry and his community. His father was a pastor, and Rick was well-regarded by all of those around him. However, Rick's home life was challenging, particularly with his relationship with his parents. His mother was aggressive and, at times, very mean-spirited; his father's passivity left Rick feeling abandoned and unsupported. This dynamic caused anger to grow inside of him as he matured, often triggering panic attacks. At times, he experienced deep rages that left him feeling guilt-ridden and ashamed.

As we worked through his struggles in a private deliverance session, Rick opened up about terrifying experiences he had endured. As a child, he often heard internal voices saying things like, "I'm going to kill you, little boy," and "I'll give you a heart attack like your dad." Another voice declared, "I am antichrist!" Rick also described seeing demons standing beside his bed that paralyzed him with fear. These experiences continued into his adulthood.

Despite these tormenting experiences, Rick was a strong believer who loved the Lord and lived a good life. However, the internal torment he faced often manifested outwardly as anxiety and panic. During our session, we uncovered a history of Freemasonry in Rick's immediate family. His ancestors had been members of the Freemason Masonic Lodge and the Eastern Star—secret societies that require blood oaths, vows of secrecy, and demonic rituals. Every level of initiation in these societies involves releasing death curses for violating their secrets and curses that are passed down through bloodlines that ultimately bring destruction to families for generations.

As we broke these generational curses in prayer, Rick experienced a profound release. The torment he had carried for so long began to leave him, and today, Rick is completely free! Although some left the church because they were uncomfortable with what was happening, testimonies like Sarah and Rick's inspired us to persevere. Their transformations and those of others like them gave us the resolve to break through into this level of freedom.

Initially, we were overwhelmed; however, we could not ignore the reality of what was happening. Every service seemed to bring manifestations of demons, regardless of the sermon's focus. Even when we taught on the love of God, demons would manifest. Many of these individuals were people we had known for years, which only deepened the shock. There was no way to "put this back in the box." We had to face this reality head-on and continue working through it while deepening our theology and diligence in searching the scriptures. As we walked with our congregation, person by person and family by family, through the process of bloodline deliverance, we witnessed the glorious freedom of Jesus manifest in their lives and in their children. It was beautiful to behold.

I vividly remember the day we realized that, finally, the majority of our congregation was free rather than demonized. It might not seem like a typical cause for celebration, but for us, it was a monumental milestone. However, as The Well continued to grow, we recognized the need to prevent adding new members who were still demonized into the fellowship. This led us to revisit and refine our membership process and covenantal commitments so that we could ensure these new members fully understood and embraced the transformational freedom available through Christ.

THE GATEWAY OF BAPTISM

Being a church that is very revival and awakening focused means that many people come to the Lord and seek baptism. Our baptismal, which is actually a cow-watering trough, is always on hand for these occasions. We often fill it with water and place it beside the altar. During worship, preaching, or other gatherings, it is not uncommon for people to come forward spontaneously and request to be baptized. We embrace this wholeheartedly, but we also realized the need to institute a process for baptism. This is because we have come to understand that just before baptism is one of the best times to cast demons out of people.

As I delved deeper into the process of baptism through the writings of many of the early church fathers, I discovered that exorcism before baptism was a common practice in the early church. In those times, baptism was often preceded by a period of preparation that lasted weeks or even months. While I am not suggesting that we must replicate that exact timeline, there are valuable principles that we can learn from this approach.

During this preparation, catechumens, those preparing for baptism, were taught the doctrines of the faith, guided in the spiritual formation, and prepared for exorcism prior to their baptism. These individuals had professed Christ and submitted to His Lordship as well as to the process of the church, but many of them came from deeply pagan backgrounds. Oftentimes, they had served and worshiped Roman gods and were now learning to follow Jesus.

As new believers, they were typically severely demonized, thus making exorcism an essential step in their baptismal preparation. Church father Hippolytus provides insight into this process, stating: "Let the catechumens be brought to the bishop by the exorcists...and let the bishop exorcise each one of them, that he may be certain they are purified."[10] In this tradition, the catechumens were brought to the bishop near the end of their preparation. The bishop would personally exorcise the demons within them to ensure they were free from demons before baptism.

Cyril of Jerusalem echoes this idea, "You were called a catechumen while you were hearing the mysteries of the faith. You were exorcised...that you might be delivered from the power of darkness."[11] Hippolytus further describes the process one went through before being baptized: "The deacon shall bring the oil of exorcism, and the bishop shall exorcise it...and deliver it to the presbyters."[12] These examples demonstrate that the early church saw exorcism as a critical aspect of the baptismal process to ensure that individuals were spiritually prepared to enter the waters of baptism.

THE BAPTISMAL PROCESS AND EXORCISM

Having membership in our faith community and being baptized are two separate things. Of course, to become a member of our fellowship community, one must be baptized. However, we often conduct baptisms spontaneously during services, so these two are not directly connected in a specific order. For example, during a service, if we open the altar for baptisms and people begin to come forward, we take time to speak with those desiring baptism before they are actually baptized. We ensure that they have repented or are repenting of their sins, that their faith is in Christ alone, and other foundational aspects typically required for baptism.

However, we still go further. We explain that many of them may still be demonized. Therefore, we ask if they or their family members have been involved in any secret societies, cults, or occult practices such as Freemasonry or witchcraft. We then lead them in renouncing these things. Even if the individuals themselves have not participated in such activities, we always include general curse-breaking prayers. We ensure they renounce Satan, all demons, his works, and any agreements that they have made with him, whether knowingly or unknowingly.

Once the renunciations are complete, we guide them in a faith commitment to Jesus. We also anoint them with oil, specifically oil of exorcism. Finally, we command the demons to flee from them. Often, demons begin to leave at that moment, but more frequently, when they come up out of the water, we proclaim over them, "All demons, come out now as the Holy Spirit fills them!" This is when most of the deliverance occurs.

The origins of this process took place during an outreach tent revival in a neighboring city. One evening, as the Spirit of God was moving powerfully across the 250 people gathered under the tent, one of our deacons brought a young woman to me. He explained that she had come to the storage lockers near the tent and felt compelled to approach after hearing the worship music coming forth from under the tent. Clearly, this was the Spirit of God drawing her. The young woman told me she wanted to give her life to Jesus and repent of her sins. This was an incredible moment, not only for her but for her family as well. However, as I looked at her, I noticed she was wearing significant demonic regalia including necklaces, bracelets, and tattoos that displayed the Eye of Horus, an Egyptian demon, as well as other symbols that revealed her involvement in the occult.

As we continued our conversation, she expressed her desire to be baptized. I explained to her that baptism would require her to renounce all former worship of false gods, divination, and occult practices. She agreed and began removing all the demonic items from her body. We led her through renouncing several things tied to her tattoos and her allegiance to these false gods. Once the curse-breaking prayers were completed, we moved her into the baptismal waters.

Immediately after she emerged from the water, demons began crying out of her in absolute agony. For the next twenty minutes, we continued casting demons out of her while she sat in the baptismal pool. Later, it was reported to me that the young woman went home and shared with her family what had happened. They were so moved by her testimony that they called the deacon, and that same night her entire family came to salvation in Jesus.

I want you to understand the importance of this story. If we had simply baptized her without addressing her renunciation of former gods and curses, she would have entered the fellowship of the saints and the household of God through faith in Christ, but her demons would have come with her. This is why it is so critical to remove the blinders and return to the original purpose of baptism: the death of the old self and also the old ways thus bringing the individual into the fullness of new life in Christ, which includes deliverance from demons.

As the apostle Peter declared on the day of Pentecost in Acts 2:38 (NRSV), *Peter said to them, 'Repent and be baptized every one of you in the name of Jesus Christ so that your sins may be forgiven, and you will receive the gift of the Holy Spirit.'* Similarly, the apostle Paul wrote in Romans 6:4 (NRSV), *Therefore we were buried with him by baptism into death, so that, just as Christ was raised from the dead by the glory of the Father, so we also might walk in newness of life.* In my opinion, this process acts as a gateway that keeps demons out of the fellowship of the saints and the household of God.

Unfortunately, we have forgotten this godly tradition and the true, spiritual significance of baptism. Instead, it has been reduced to a superficial exercise, where children with little to no understanding view it as a fun thing to do because their friends are being baptized. We must return to the biblical power and experience of baptism, not just the doctrine of it, but the transformative encounter it was always meant to be.

CHAPTER 3

ANCIENT COSMOLOGY WORLDVIEW

A SUPERNATURAL WORLDVIEW

Demons are a widely discussed topic of modern Christianity with varying opinions as to what they are, where they came from, how they function, and how to make them leave. There are many books and ministers today that write about deliverance ministry, define demons, and how to be free from bondages. However, many of these books are written purely on an intellectual level and lack the practical experience of actually casting out demons on both a personal and a regional or national level.

Before discussing any further, this book is written on the foundation that demons do still exist and function in the modern world just as they did all throughout biblical history. Additionally, the understanding of the ancient biblical worldview must be discussed. To study the scriptures without first understanding the supernatural worldview in which they were written is simply ignorant. The modern worldview is drastically different from the biblical worldview.

BIBLICAL TRANSLATIONS

The Bible describes a supernatural world that is foreign to many modern Christians. Most believers in the modern era fail to understand the ancient cosmological understanding that the scriptures were written upon, thus losing the context of many biblical stories and passages. As a result, many modern Bible translations have changed the supernatural language of scripture to fit the context of the modern, intellectual worldview that is explained solely by science and human logic. Further, most translations have even removed the proper names of demonic entities that are stated in both the Old Testament and the New Testament and changed them to fit a modern worldview and contemporary context.

Without a proper understanding of the ancient cosmology, many modern translations fail to capture the fullness of the Bible as well as the theological implications that come from this understanding. Further, there will never be a complete understanding of the spiritual world in which Christians live today without this understanding. As a result, many in the church today are living from a defeatist, victim mentality and not fully assuming the victorious role and authority that Jesus has given His church and all believers in the New Covenant. We are not on the defense just waiting on attacks from the enemy, but we are called to live on the offense and bring the battle to the gates of hell!

ANCIENT COSMOLOGY

"Cosmology refers to the way we understand the structure of the universe."[13] Postmodernism has greatly affected the views of the Western world today, especially how our society translates the universe and its structure and thus, how we relate to it. The basic tenets of postmodernism address what is a reality in the realms of knowledge and what is taught as being real.[14] This is why absolute truth sourced solely from God and His Word is crucial; in the modern era, truth is being challenged and adapted to fit each person's own convictions or beliefs. This is dangerous; the results are evidenced throughout our society and through much of American culture.

There is clearly a search for supernatural experience, but sadly, it is often being sought after through science, self-enlightenment, New Age practices, yoga, and other outlets, most of which are sourced in the demonic world. Even entertainment is inundated with this spiritual fascination. The Barna Group has performed multiple studies over the past two decades, which have provided the following results concerning the supernatural experience of the younger generation *within* the modern church.

Only 28 percent of young adults ages 12 to 29 recall receiving any teaching on the supernatural realm within the past year. While 79 percent of this same group believe in some form of an immaterial, spiritual world, over 50 percent could not articulate a structure for this universe. Only 58 percent believed that Satan and demons exist at all but did not identify them as enemies of God, yet 89 percent professed a belief in angels. The trends revealed that many in this generation have adopted a belief in what they view as "good" concerning the spiritual realm and reject the notions of evil in this same world.

Thus, the fruits of this belief have created a staggering trend of experimentation in the spiritual world without understanding the consequences or risks associated with it. In this group, 81 percent of Protestants stated they had experimented or engaged in spiritual activities outside the church such as psychic readings, tarot cards, Ouija boards, divinations, séances, occult practices, and other forms of witchcraft. There is an increasing trend that this generation is willing to accept what is viewed as "good" in the spiritual realm while ignoring the "evil" that exists as well.[15]

The modern trends in entertainment would further this desire for spirituality with the precept of accepting what is deemed "good" but denying that which is perceived as "evil."

SUPERNATURAL OBSESSION THROUGH ENTERTAINMENT

In the last couple of years, there has been a surge in spiritual movies that have hit records in theaters and through streaming devices. The *Beetlejuice* movies would be one such example categorized as comedic horror.[16] The essence of this series is a mischievous demon who comes back from the dead to haunt people by seducing them to say his name three times, which summons him back from the underworld. With the mixture of comedy, *Beetlejuice* has been widely accepted by many Christians as simply comedic entertainment.

In 2023, the rerelease of the *Hocus Pocus* movie from 1993 grossed over $5 million in its opening weekend.[17] This movie series is produced by Disney as a "family-friendly Halloween ghost story" rated PG, meaning it is appropriate for most children with only some parental guidance suggested. The plot is about three witches who were summoned back to life by a teenage boy accidentally. The three witches desire to lure children to their home to "drink their life from them."[18] The movie is full of curses, potions, and other wicked witchcraft practices.

Another movie that has surged in popularity in 2024 is the remake of the musical *Wicked.* Good witches and bad witches are the primary characters, making the idea of witchcraft seem harmless. Glinda, the good witch of Oz, asks the question, "Are people born wicked? Or do they have wickedness thrust upon them?"[19] The emotion of the film is to challenge if a witch has to be evil or could they actually be good, and truly, what defines good from evil anyways?

Sadly, many have fallen into the deception of these trends as mere entertainment and have opened doors for themselves to accept evil as good and thus, reject the true reality of the demonic world. Additionally, all of these movies are targeting children and families, further producing a fascination with the spiritual world but through demonic access. These forms of entertainment are causing a generation to be challenged that evil is not truly "wicked," but can also be good, and witchcraft practices are harmless or just fun to experiment with. This could be a visual description of the prophet Isaiah's warning in Isaiah 5:20: "*Woe to those who call evil good, and good evil; who substitute darkness for light and light for darkness; who substitute bitter for sweet and sweet for bitter!*"

From the Barna Group's research, it is evident that the deficit and neglect of the supernatural world being taught in the church have caused the younger generations to seek out an understanding of the spiritual world outside of God and instead, through the demonic world. These generations are being indoctrinated by demons while much of the modern church is busy arguing over when the world is going to end and just holding on until Jesus returns. There must be a restoration in modern Christian theology, especially within the church, that teaches and embraces a spiritual worldview.

WHAT ARE DEMONS? THREE MODERN VIEWS

This is a loaded question that many have attempted to answer for centuries. There are many opinions that attempt to define, "What is a demon?" One view is that of fallen angels, which is the most common view in Evangelicalism today. This view comes from Luke 10:18: "*And He said to them, 'I watched Satan fall from heaven like lightning.*'" This view is further supported by Revelation 12:7-9:

> *And there was war in heaven, Michael and his angels waging war with the dragon. The dragon and his angels waged war, and they did not prevail, and there was no longer a place found for them in heaven. And the great dragon was thrown down, the serpent of old who is called the devil and Satan, who deceives the whole world; he was thrown down to the earth, and his angels were thrown down with him.*

Another view is that demons are disembodied Nephilim. Dr. Michael Heiser supports this view. The primary scripture to support this comes from Genesis 6:1-4:

> *Now it came about, when mankind began to multiply on the face of the land, and daughters were born to them, that the sons of God saw that the daughters of mankind were beautiful; and they took wives for themselves, whomever they chose. Then the Lord said, "My Spirit will not remain with man forever, because he is also flesh; nevertheless his days shall be*

> *120 years." The Nephilim were on the earth in those days, and also afterward, when the sons of God came in to the daughters of mankind, and they bore children to them. Those were the mighty men who were of old, men of renown.*

This view argues that the serpent who deceived Eve in the Garden of Eden was a spirit, not a natural snake. Genesis 3:15 describes the descendants of Eve would be at war with the offspring of the serpent: "*And I will make enemies of you and the woman, and of your offspring and her Descendant; He shall bruise you on the head, and you shall bruise Him on the heel.*" This view connects Jesus's rebuke of the Pharisees in Matthew 23:33 to further support this claim: "*You snakes, you offspring of vipers, how will you escape the sentence of hell* [Gehenna]?" Jesus further describes the Pharisees as sons of the devil in John 8:44, giving implications from Genesis: "*You are of your father the devil, and you want to do the desires of your father. He was a murderer from the beginning, and does not stand in the truth because there is no truth in him. Whenever he tells a lie, he speaks from his own nature, because he is a liar and the father of lies.*" Therefore, in this view, demons are the spirits that corrupted humanity as the seeds of Satan, which came through the reproduction between the spiritual Nephilim and humanity.

A third view is that before the creation of Adam, there was a pre-Adamic race that God created but not in His own likeness or image. This race rebelled against Him and aligned with Satan and his fallen angels who were cast out of heaven due to their rebellion. As a result, the world was destroyed. All of this is believed to have occurred between Genesis 1:1 and Genesis 1:2. According to this view, this accounts for the state of the world being "formless and void" at the beginning of Genesis 1:2 since it had just been completely destroyed and was about to be recreated. This race was stripped of their physical bodies and became disembodied spirits which they refer to as "demons." As a result, they are constantly searching for a body to inhabit according to Luke 11:24-26.

While each of these have strengths and weaknesses, ultimately, scripture does not provide the specific answer to this question. What scripture does emphatically answer, though, is that demons are evil, spiritual beings; God is supreme in power and authority over all of them; and finally, Jesus cast them out, and commanded us to do the same. At the end of the day, these are the principles that we stand on.

THE SONS OF GOD

Scripture does provide insights into the understanding of ruling, territorial spirits that would be described as principalities. These are distinctly different from demons that are cast out of individuals, but understanding these spirits will help provide a further framework for deliverance ministry. First, let's look at the Hebrew understanding of the Sons of God or the *elohim*. Understanding the Sons of God in both title and function provides the framework for a biblical worldview as well as an understanding of demons that impacts both deliverance ministry and spiritual warfare. Many modern translations of scripture have changed the supernatural language of the Bible to fit a cessationist or natural-human understanding.

Elohim is a formal title in Hebrew used exclusively as a name of God; there are over 2,000 references to this name of God.[20] However, there is another form of this Hebrew word used as a generic "god," which is used in both singular and plural forms. It is often translated as angels, sons of God, heavenly beings, spirits, hosts, or gods. These spiritual beings, in all forms, reside in the spiritual realm but interact with the natural earthly realm.[21] As spirits, these entities "by nature, are not embodied, at least in the sense of our human experience of being physical in form."[22] The Old Testament writers used the language of "spirit" to contrast the natural realm of humanity. As spiritual beings, then, the plural usage of *elohim* is understood to refer to "a populated spiritual world."[23]

THE DIVINE COUNCIL OF GOD

In the Old Testament, God had a Divine Council that was made up of these *elohim*. This is described in Deuteronomy 32, 1 Kings 22:19-23, Psalm 82, and Daniel 7.[24] The purpose of this divine council was not to tell God what to do or make decisions for Him, but rather "the council served only to reemphasize and execute His decisions."[25] The title that is most accurate to translate the plural *elohim* is the Sons of God.

Deuteronomy 32 and Psalm 82 provide the framework for this understanding. Deuteronomy 32:8-9 states:

> *When the Most High gave the nations their inheritance, when He separated the sons of Adam, He set the boundaries of the peoples according to the number of the sons of God. For the Lord's portion is His people; Jacob is the allotment of His inheritance.*

In these verses, God Most High has disinherited the nations of the earth and assigned dominion to the *elohim* as the Sons of God; He separated Israel apart from the rest of the nations as His own inheritance. In their corruption and rebellion, the

Sons of God enslaved the people and ruled with injustice. They caused the nations to worship them as gods, and at times, even ancient Israel fell into this same trap of idolatry by worshiping the "gods" of other nations.[26] Deuteronomy 4:19-20 supports this interpretation:

> *And be careful not to raise your eyes to heaven and look at the sun, the moon, and the stars, all the heavenly lights, and allow yourself to be drawn away and worship them and serve them, things which the Lord your God has allotted to all the peoples under the whole heaven. But the Lord has taken you and brought you out of the iron furnace, from Egypt, to be a people of His own possession, as today.*

Psalm 82 explains that the Sons of God rebelled against Him and became corrupt, causing God's created order of the world to be thrown into chaos.[27]

Scholar Clinton Arnold translates the *elohim* to be fallen guardian angels, which he states could be called demons.[28] His support comes from the Septuagint translation of Psalm 96:5, "*For all the gods of the nations are demons, but the Lord made the heavens.*"[29] Deuteronomy 32:17 states that Israel embraced the gods of the nations and sacrificed to demons in their idolatry.[30] In conclusion, Arnold argues that in the Old Testament, "Demons stand behind the idol worship and animate it as part of their attempt to subvert the plan of God and seek worship for themselves."[31] The Hebrew word translated as "demon" is only used three times in the Old Testament,[32] but in function, the disobedient *elohim* are connected to the demonic entities that were still operating all throughout the New Testament.

RESISTING IDOLATRY

The temptation of Israel was always to worship idols or the gods of the nations rather than God Most High. It is important to note that the designation of the Sons of God does not describe the act of polytheism;[33] Israel was a monotheistic nation. The call to worship their one true God is found in Deuteronomy 6:4: "*Hear, O Israel, the LORD our God, the LORD is one!*" Jews today still recite this passage twice daily as a confession called the Shema. This passage affirms Israel's triune God as well as the nation's radical, monotheistic faith.

The holy identity of ancient Israel was that they were a people separated for God by God who were to worship only God alone. Comparatively, the nations of the earth worshiped many gods, which made Israel unique as a monotheistic nation. This same concept is evidenced today as well. Many nations of the world worship a multitude of gods, but the distinction of Christianity is that Christians are called to worship *only* the one, true God.

DEUTERONOMY 32

A deeper dive into Deuteronomy 32 provides an important piece in understanding the *elohim* and their roles in the created world. Deuteronomy 32:17 states, "*They* [the Israelites] *sacrificed to demons* [shedim], *who were not God* [eloah], *to gods* [elohim] *whom they have not known, new gods who came lately, whom your fathers did not know.*" The Hebrew term *shedim* is also used in Psalm 106:37 and is translated as "demons." This word comes from the ancient Near Eastern Akkadian word, *shedu,* which was defined as a protective, guardian spirit-being.[34]

"In the context of Deuteronomy 32:17, *shedim* were elohim—spirit beings guarding foreign territory—who must not be worshiped."[35] Their roles were to guard or protect their assigned territory and the people within that territory on behalf of God. However, not all of them stayed true to their assignment, and many rebelled against it. The key of this passage is to understand that the *elohim* had specific, territorial assignments given by God to guard and rule over regions and nations. We will discuss this more in Chapter 4.

PSALM 82

Psalm 82 adds another important piece to understanding *elohim* as it is used four times in this psalm. The language of the psalm fits similar language used for judicial procedure throughout the book of Psalms.[36] The Old Testament prophets also use similar language for judicial procedure.[37] The first usage is found in verse 1: "*God* [Elohim] *takes His position in His assembly; He judges in the midst of the gods* [elohim]." The first usage is commonly agreed upon by most scholars to refer to the title of Yahweh; the second usage in verse 1 is a common point of disagreement.[38] Verses 2-5 describe the judgments of these *elohim,* which has caused injustice among the people. Those who have suffered the most from these governing gods are the weak, afflicted, needy, and destitute of society. As a result, the people live in darkness.

Verses 6-7 address the *elohim* again: *"I said, 'You are gods* [elohim], *and all of you are sons of the Most High. Nevertheless you will die like men, and fall like one of the princes.'"* The address is made to the same "gods" as mentioned in verse 2 for their failure to execute justice and rule righteously. Therefore, verse 6 must be referring to spiritual beings rather than humans as the punishment for their actions is mortality; humanity is not immortal in nature so this would be no further punishment if applied to human rulers, kings, or judges.

For this reason, scholar Julian Morgenstern states that *elohim* in verse 6 "cannot effectively refer to earthly kings or rulers, even those who called themself 'god.'"[39] The usage of "princes" in verse 7 correlates to Daniel 10:13 as the prince of the kingdom of Persia opposed Daniel for twenty-one days; one of the chief princes of God, Michael, came to help Daniel in his spiritual battle. These princes were spiritual beings, not natural men. By opposing both God and his servant Daniel, the prince of Persia was clearly a demonic entity, but his title also implies being a territorial spirit.

The final *elohim* is used in verse 8: "*Arise, God* [Elohim], *judge the earth! For You possess all the nations.*" The psalmist brings this oracle full circle by addressing Yahweh again as *Elohim*, the same address as used in verse 1. God alone will judge the other *elohim* who have been corrupted and have rebelled against Him by promising them death like mere humans and the loss of their immortality as spiritual beings.

OTHER REFERENCES TO ELOHIM

Psalm 8:4-5 uses the plural *elohim* to compare the role of humans in the natural created order: *"What is man that You think of him, and a son of man that You are concerned about him? Yet You have made him a little lower than God* [Elohim], *and You crown him with glory and majesty!"* While the New American Standard Bible translates this elohim as a title name for God or as angels, this passage fits the same interpretation as Psalm 82 with the understanding of the "Sons of God." In the created order, Yahweh is over and above all of creation. Below Him, the *elohim*, as sons of God, were positioned to rule and guard the nations. Humans are created a little lower than the *elohim* but still are crowned with glory and majesty as they are created in the image of God.

Psalm 29 also follows this same guide for interpreting *elohim*. The opening call to worship in verse 1 addresses the plural *elohim*: "*Ascribe to the Lord, sons of the mighty* [elohim], *Ascribe to the Lord glory and strength. Ascribe to the Lord the glory due His name; Worship the Lord in holy attire.*" The progression through this psalm begins with the call to worship from the Sons of God followed by the voice of the Lord throughout all of creation, including the elements of nature and animals, and finally, culminates in an exclamation at the end of verse 9: "*And in His temple everything says, 'Glory!'*"

In the context of Psalm 29:1, scholar Tremper Longman states, "The worship of God has its greatest momentum when God's creatures, both in heaven and on earth, join to praise him."[40] The psalm concludes by moving from the *elohim* to all of creation, and finally, addresses humanity following the pattern of the creation narrative in Genesis 1. The strength of God mentioned in verse 1 is now imparted to humanity in verse 9 as a bestowing from the divine realm to the human realm, the heavenly realm to the earthly realm.

Psalm 97:9 provides another understanding of the *elohim* and their relation to God: "*For You are the Lord Most High over all the earth; You are exalted far above all gods* [elohim]." The Lord Most High is the name of God, Yahweh ⊠Elyôn. This title is also used in Deuteronomy 32:8-9 to designate specifically that the Lord Most High is over all other gods and every other heavenly being, including the *elohim*.

CHAPTER 4

THE ROLES AND ASSIGNMENTS OF THE *ELOHIM*

THE TOWER OF BABEL

Genesis 10–11 containing the table of nations and the Tower of Babel story provide the background to the *elohim* and their assigned roles in the created world. Deuteronomy 32:8-9 describes the events of Babel in which the Lord scattered the people for attempting to build a tower that reached the heavens in order to make a name for themselves, not for God. They also violated the command of God to scatter and fill the earth in Genesis 1:28. Heiser identifies one significant link between Genesis 10–11 and Deuteronomy 32 with the usage for the Hebrew word translated "separation" speaking of God separating the nations.[41]

Further, when God dispersed the people, He also disinherited the nations keeping only Israel for Himself.[42] Israel was not counted in the table of nations containing 70 nations as she was separate.[43] Verse 9 specifically implies a contrast between Israel being the inheritance of the Lord while the other nations are not: "*For the Lord's portion is His people; Jacob is the allotment of His inheritance.*" Further, this verse intends ownership over the people.[44]

The sequence of this passage is important as the Babel narrative occurred before God made his covenant with Abraham in Genesis 12:1-3.

THE VICTORY OF JESUS AS THE SON OF GOD

Now that the Old Testament usage of the Sons of God has been evaluated, the New Testament understanding must begin with Jesus as *the* Son of God. Jesus Christ came to the earth and is given the title, "The Son of God." Satan was the first entity to recognize this title during the temptation of Jesus in Matthew 4:3 and 6. The demons in the two men in Gadarenes also recognize and cry out to Jesus as the Son of God. Mark 3:11 and 5:7 record the demon's recognition of Jesus as the Son of God. Simon Peter has this incredible revelation of Jesus in Matthew 16:16 as discussed previously. Even the centurion and guards of His tomb recognize Jesus as the Son of God when the earth quaked and the tombs opened upon His death in Matthew 27:54.

Luke 1:32 and 35 provide another important aspect of Jesus's sonship: He is the Son of God Most High; He is not just one of many "Sons" of God, but He is "The" Son of God. Therefore, He is above all of the *elohim* as the Sons of God. In Luke's genealogy of Jesus, he distinctively traces His family lineage back to Adam, as the Son of God: "*the son of Enosh, the son of Seth, the son of Adam, the son of God.*" Luke's writing also affirms this authority by using the same name, God Most High, as used in Deuteronomy 32:8-9 and Psalm 82:6. Jesus as the Son of God is part of the Trinity. This doctrine is essential to the Christian faith: "The Triune God is one God who exists eternally as three infinite, eternal, interpenetrating Persons: Father, Son, and Holy Spirit."[45]

PAULINE THEOLOGY CONCERNING ELOHIM

It is clear that the Old Testament and ancient Israel understood the Sons of God and their role, which is a present theme throughout the Bible. In the New Testament, Paul frequently addresses spiritual powers of darkness and principalities. Scholar F.F. Bruce states that these powers refer to "the deep, cosmic, demonic personal realities capturing structures and society and people in this world systemically to thwart the good plan of God."[46] Similarly to the previous descriptions of the *elohim* of the Old Testament, in correlation with Colossians 2, scholar G.B. Caird states:

> In its natural state the human race lives in bondage not only to sin, death, and the Law, but to a host of angelic beings, whose varied nomenclature indicates that all in common have been invested by God with a species of authority over the created order, though somehow the authority becomes corrupt and demonic. These powers include the guardians of the pagan state, the mediators of the Torah, and the angels who preside over the national order—the heavenly representatives of civil, religious, and natural law.[47]

While a variety of names are used to describe these powers,[48] it is important to recognize that all of them are similar in both character and function to the *elohim* of the Old Testament. In character, these powers "are antagonistic to the temporal causes of God and his people."[49] In function, these powers were also given temporary rule over the nations by Yahweh.[50] Further, the apostle Paul was a trained scholar of Israel's history, the scriptures, and their traditions as he was a devout Jew before his conversion and trained at the feet of the great teacher, Gamaliel.[51] Paul would have understood the supernatural worldview of the ancient world which was the backdrop for his writings in the New Testament. Regardless of the title used in the New Testament to describe these powers, the point is always the same: Christ is exalted and victorious over all of them.

Dr. Ronn Johnson makes a strong argument that Paul interpreted the death, resurrection, and ascension of Christ to fulfill the divine council scene of Daniel 7, and thus, the climax of the New Testament is the absolute victory over these powers.[52] Colossians 1:16 further reveals Paul's view on these invisible, spiritual powers: they were created by God, through God, and for God. In Christ, these powers have been defeated and their authority revoked, but they still battle with Christians until their full defeat at the final return of Christ.[53] This furthers the Old Testament's understanding of the *elohim* as stated previously: spiritual beings created by God and given rule over territories and people. Colossians 2:13-15 states:

> *And when you were dead in your wrongdoings and the uncircumcision of your flesh, He made you alive together with Him, having forgiven us all our wrongdoings, having canceled the certificate of debt consisting of decrees against us, which was hostile to us; and He has taken it out of the way, having nailed it to the cross. When He had disarmed the rulers and authorities, He made a public display of them, having triumphed over them through Him.*

These powers have been defeated in Christ in the past tense. However, "the structures are still at work, so it is in the church that this defeat is to be embodied."[54] The sign to reveal to the authorities and rulers of darkness that their power is revoked is discovered in the mystery of Christ: when there is true unity in the church (Ephesians 3:3-7). This is the foundation for the modern church and its mission still today.

VISIBLE EFFECTS OF THE *ELOHIM*: HAITI

Since these demonic spiritual entities are territorial, they affect not only the people who reside in a geographical location, but also the land itself. This explains why when we cross from one geographical area into another, we often will discern spiritual distinctions. Think of driving from one town and crossing into the next. Have you ever felt like something was different? Maybe the next town felt peaceful or restful; maybe it felt dark and scary. Regardless, these discernments can be the result of the effects of the territorial demonic spirits in operation.

The greatest example that I have seen of the effects on the land is to look at the nation of Haiti. From a bird's-eye view, Haiti forms the western side of the island of Hispaniola with the Dominican Republic forming the eastern side. On a satellite view without any borders drawn, you see the line between these two nations. The Dominican Republic is a lush, tropical environment with dense trees, jungles, and a multitude of natural resources as well as a diverse ecosystem with a wide variety of plants and animals. In contrast, Haiti has been almost completely deforested revealing barren mountains and dry land. There are hardly any natural resources left on the western side of this island. The nation has very few native animal species that live here anymore because of the lack of a livable habitat. Why is this?

Haiti used to be known as the "Pearl of the Caribbean" for its natural beauty, especially on its beaches; now, it is the poorest nation in the Western Hemisphere and in the top five globally.

Studying Haiti's history reveals the answer to this question. Haiti became the first successful slave-nation in the world to gain its independence through an uprising. In 1804, the slaves successfully overtook their captors, the Spanish and the French, during this revolt. The Spanish retreated to the eastern side of the island, which is now the Dominican Republic. Upon this great victory, the slaves held a historic voodoo ceremony and dedicated their side of the island to Satan through a massive ritual that involved the slaughter of a multitude of pigs and other animals as blood sacrifices. This ritual also involved demonic worship that used an oversized voodoo drum. I learned this not from a history book, but through personal experience while visiting the Haitian National Museum in the capital city of Port-au-Prince on multiple occasions. This exact voodoo drum is at the center of this museum along with the description of this ceremony; it towers at least six feet tall and is a sign of Haiti's national freedom from slavery.

However, dedicating the land to Satan came with great consequences. The Haitian people came into agreement with a wicked, territorial principality and further, made sacrifices and dedications of their land to this demonic entity. The effects of this act are visible, even on a map. This also accounts for the turmoil that has plagued Haiti for many decades. From murderous dictators to disease and death to a nation in absolute chaos, as of 2024, the nation is still currently in great turmoil and without a president or any functioning government; the gangs have completely taken over the capital city which accounts for over 20 percent of the nation's entire population. Many hospitals and schools have been forced to close due to safety. The US Embassy closed down a few years ago and US citizens were advised to leave and to not travel to the nation. Even the Port-au-Prince airport remains closed at this time, making travel in and out of the nation nearly impossible. Many have fled and sought refuge in the countryside and rural areas, but tragically, many people are suffering and in great need of help. The entire nation is a visible example of the impacts of ruling, demonic principalities as well as a nation that desperately needs deliverance, for both the people and the land. My heart grieves for the state of the nation as we continue to pray and intercede for God's salvation, deliverance, and healing.

CHAPTER 5

HIDDEN "GODS" OF THE BIBLE

UNIQUE POINTS OF BLOODLINE DELIVERANCE

Over many years of deliverance ministry, I have examined and applied various methodologies for setting people free. First and foremost, I want to emphasize that methodologies themselves do not set people free—it is only through faith in Jesus and applying the authority, power, and truth of God's Word that brings freedom. However, I am not opposed to methodologies; they are systems we create to make deliverance reproducible and teachable and thus, empower others to carry out the ministry of Jesus.

Let me be clear: the ultimate method to employ is the leading of the Holy Spirit in each moment. For example, in the methodology of bloodline deliverance, we follow a 15-step process. If I am on step four of the process, and the Holy Spirit leads me in a specific direction, I will always follow His lead. Anything else would be disobedient and unwise. After addressing what the Holy Spirit reveals, then I return to step four and proceed with the process. After doing thousands of exorcisms, my teams and I have learned to be extremely thorough. Demons are manipulative and scheming. They always seek to maintain bloodline curses and continue their work within families; they will attempt to hide or deceive in order to fulfill their demonic agenda.

I understand that many of you may already have your own approach to deliverance or have been introduced to different methodologies. I completely celebrate anyone who is actively doing deliverance ministry. My goal here is not to oppose but to enhance through offering insights and techniques that could make your ministry more effective, thorough, and capable of addressing even complex deliverance situations.

Before I began to understand the four areas of bloodline deliverance, I saw about 60 percent of the people I ministered to get set free from demons. While I celebrated that 60 percent, I was heartbroken over the remaining 40 percent who did not experience breakthrough. This drove me on a determined quest to understand more. I firmly believe that Jesus and the covenant He established are entirely sufficient for the restoration of every person and family. Out of love, compassion, and dedication to the truth of God's Word, I persevered. Through this process, I discovered these specific four areas, and as a result, we now see a much higher success rate in deliverance ministry.

I also want to introduce the concept of spiritual intelligence in deliverance; it is crucial that we understand how it applies to individuals, families, bloodlines, cities, regions, and beyond. While God cares deeply about setting the individual free, deliverance often has implications far beyond one single person. When addressing demons, breaking curses, and freeing bloodlines, we must think beyond the individual and recognize that the insights we gain during a deliverance session can have a ripple effect on entire families, communities, and even regions. This broader perspective requires what I call apostolic thinking. The person in front of you is not just an individual needing freedom but often, the entry point for their entire family's deliverance. I call these individuals Curse Breakers—those who are invited by God to step into a level of freedom that surpasses anything their family has previously experienced. This is an invitation extended to everyone, though not all have the faith or confidence to step into it.

SPIRITUAL INTELLIGENCE

Bloodline Deliverance revealed an unexpected concept—spiritual intelligence. While Jesus cares deeply about individual freedom, deliverance sessions often unveil insights into regional strongholds and demonic structures. For instance, during one session, an assistant working with me began manifesting after we completed a three-hour deliverance. A demon spoke through him, declaring, "I am Anubis, and this region belongs to me." Anubis, the Egyptian god of death, seemed an unlikely entity to manifest in East Tennessee. As we delved deeper, we found a connection between Anubis and the Masonic Lodge in our area, revealing a territorial link to demonic oppression. We have learned the value of brief interrogations during deliverance to discern a demon's name and function. Using this intelligence, we have diagrammed demonic kingdoms and identified structures holding bloodlines and territories in bondage.

Concerning spiritual intelligence and apostolic thinking, imagine going into a region or territory to minister deliverance. I may not know much about the area initially, but if my team and I minister to 50 people and 40 of them manifest demons connected to the ancient Aztec pantheon, we gain critical spiritual intelligence. This tells us that many of the families in that territory are likely direct descendants of the Aztec Empire, and those curses that are connected to the worship of false gods have remained active in their bloodlines for centuries. This often occurs even among Christians because curses are not automatically broken. Just as salvation is received by faith, curses must also be broken through the application of faith in Christ's authority, power, and grace. We will delve deeper into this concept in Chapter 7 concerning curses and curse-breaking.

Similarly, if I minister in an area with a predominantly European population of Nordic descent, we frequently see manifestations tied to ancient Nordic demons. These may include Odin, Thor, Loki, Fenrir, Freya, and others. Over years of ministering in hundreds of territories, we have compiled extensive spiritual intelligence that allows us to minister more effectively and thoroughly.

For example, I recently returned from Paraguay. As I entered a specific territory, I conducted practical research about the false gods worshiped by the indigenous people before Christianity was introduced. Quickly, I discovered a demonic trinity: a sun god, a moon goddess, and what I call an "evil enforcer," a pattern often found in many indigenous cultures. These figures may have different names based upon the culture but they operate and function similarly.

In Paraguay, I identified the sun god as Tupa, the moon goddess as Arasy or Jaci, and the enforcer as Tua. Based on this research, I wrote basic renunciations and began leading people through them during services. On the first night, with about 100 people present, 15 to 20 manifested demons identified as witchcraft. While witchcraft was not one of the named deities, it represented the system of power that kept people in bondage to these gods. The spiritual intelligence gained from that meeting revealed that we needed to break the power of witchcraft to penetrate deeper and set the people free.

THE CASE OF ANYA

During a session with a middle-aged woman, a demon manifested with a defiant smirk but remained silent and unresponsive. Knowing her bloodline was Irish, I researched Irish deities during a break and came across Anya, a goddess associated with seduction and red hair. When I mentioned the name, the woman was shocked. She confessed that before becoming a Christian, she used the name Anya when frequenting bars and engaging in sexual promiscuity. Moreover, she would dye her hair red during those times, unknowingly embodying the characteristics of the demon.

As I led her through renunciations concerning possible ties with this particular demon, immediately, Anya manifested and revealed an ancient bloodline curse going back to her ancestors in Ireland. Once this curse of witchcraft and sexual perversion was broken, the demon lost its hold. We bound it all together and cast it out. This revelation demonstrated how deeply demons can disciple individuals, shaping behaviors, physical attributes, and identities. Recognizing and confronting these spiritual influences is crucial for true freedom.

THE HIDDEN "GODS" OF THE BIBLE

The Bible describes a spiritual world that is often overlooked due to modern English translations that fail to identify and capture this spiritual world. Many skeptics of deliverance ministry struggle with the idea of naming specific demons or principalities. This will be discussed much deeper in Chapter 9, but identifying demons by name is very helpful in the deliverance process. When dealing with principalities, this same practice is also of equal importance. This concept is rooted in scripture as many demonic entities are actually identified in the Bible through their proper names. By identifying them by name, whether in individual deliverance or through strategic-level warfare, this provides spiritual intelligence and context to demonic structures, hierarchies, cultural contexts, characteristics of these entities, and how they function together.

It is also important to identify the locations of these named entities. Through the ancient worldview of three realms—heavenly, earthly, and underworld—further insights can be gained as to how these spirits operate and function in their realms. The ancient wilderness location is also of significance in this discussion as it was known for being the place where many of these evil spirits ruled and reigned.

Theologian Harold Eberle makes a strong distinction when discussing the structure of the universe and the understanding of these three realms interacting with each other. The Platonic worldview, developed by the philosophers, including Plato, views two distinctive and separate worlds that do not interact with each other: the world of ideals and thought versus the natural, earthly realm.[55] The era of Enlightenment was focused on how to remain in the "Platonic world" built upon science, reason, knowledge, and logic and thus, to separate oneself from the carnality and imperfections of the earthly realm. This has greatly influenced the modern Western worldview, which often rejects much of the spiritual realm since it is often supernatural, meaning beyond natural means. In contrast, the Hebrew-Biblical worldview "recognizes God's spiritual realms as very close to and even filling the same space as the natural realm."[56] These realms were not separate but continually engaging with each other at various levels. This is the worldview of the Bible.

THREE REALM WORLDVIEW

The ancient cosmology structure of the Bible consists of three realms: the heavenly realm, the earthly realm, and the underworld. All of these realms are included in the Creation story from Genesis 1. While these three realms are distinct, they are constantly engaging with each other in various capacities. Let's briefly look at each realm and how they are described in scripture.

HEAVENLY REALM

The heavenly realm is first described in the creation narrative of Genesis 1:6-8 as "the expanse" in the sky above the waters. Often translated as "the heavens," this place was the domain of God where He dwelled alongside His heavenly council and other heavenly beings such as angels and the elohim.[57] According to Exodus 20:4, the ancient worldview believed that this heavenly realm existed above the earthly realm structurally. The boundary between this heavenly realm and the earthly realm below was viewed as "the boundary between light and darkness."[58] The foundations that upheld this realm were often viewed as the highest mountain peaks that penetrated the sky into this glorious realm.[59] Scripture also states that this heavenly realm contained doors, windows, and gates which could flow down from heaven to earth releasing rain, water, and the contents of storehouses.[60] The heavenly realm contained the fullness and overwhelming abundance of the glory and goodness of God.

Another lie that has penetrated much of the church is that this heavenly realm is only accessible after someone dies. This was not the same view as described in scripture. Now, in the New Covenant and through the Holy Spirit, *all* believers have access to this realm in Christ. Paul frequently discusses this access for all in Jesus. The apostles and the early church lived their lives through the empowerment of the Holy Spirit after Acts 2, which resulted in the many miracles, signs, and wonders that marked the early church.

This is the primary reason the Western church today looks so vastly different from the church as described in Acts. Instead, many in the church have believed a lie that they are only waiting on the day that they can access this heavenly realm, and therefore, they are not functioning in the power and promises that Jesus gave to them. Upon His ascension, Jesus clearly stated in Matthew 28:19 that, "*All authority has been given to Me in heaven and on earth.*" Now, we have that same authority as ambassadors of Christ to go to the nations and bring heaven to earth, just as Jesus did in His own earthly ministry.

The Greek word for "heavenly places" is the adjective, *epouranios*. This word means "above the sky, celestial, heavenly."[61] It is primarily used in the New Testament by Paul and the author of Hebrews. The books of Ephesians and Hebrews account for 11 of the 17 verses in the entire New Testament that use this word.[62] Ephesians will further be discussed later for its emphasis on the supernatural world and how Christians are called to live in it. Hebrews emphasizes the access to this realm in the New

Covenant through Jesus and by the Holy Spirit. There is access to this heavenly realm now in Christ.

EARTHLY REALM

The earthly realm is located just below the heavenly realm and was referred to initially as "the waters below."[63] It is surrounded by the sea and had risen from out of the water as dry land.[64] The ancient world understood the earthly realm to be anchored and fixed in place by pillars or sunken foundations.[65] This realm is the domain of humanity and natural forms of life, including animals and vegetation. Scripture typically translates this realm as earth or land. Genesis 1:1 makes a clear distinction between the heavenly realm and the earthly realm. Further, in Genesis 1:28, God gives humanity the rule and dominion of this natural realm.

THE UNDERWORLD

The underworld was understood to be the land of the dead, which was structurally viewed as below the earthly realm. The most frequent name used for this location in the Old Testament is *Sheol*.[66] *Sheol* was the "mirror-opposition" to the heavenly realms of God revealing a polarity between the created order of God in the heavenlies and the chaotic, evil disorder of the underworld below.[67] The death graves dug by men represented the gateways to the underworld.[68] Both Job and Jonah provide additional understanding of this world. Job 26:5-6 describes this "realm of the dead" in watery terminology and as being naked and exposed of all covering. Jonah associates his time in the belly of the whale as similar to the underworld, which included watery deeps at the bottom of the mountains with a pit containing bars that closed forever.[69]

It is important to note that while there is a clearly defined, three-tiered structure for these three realms, there is also a spiritual and a natural side to each one. For example, there is a spiritual, heavenly realm as well as a natural heavenly realm that is visible when we look into the skies. In the earthly realm, we live in a natural structure but also are engaged with spiritual entities that reside and function in this realm. The same is true for the underworld.

INTRODUCTION

As we begin discussing the "gods" of various realms, it is important to understand that we are referring to territorial principalities—the rebellious sons of God or the *elohim*—who turned against God and were dethroned of their seated positions. These spiritual beings seek to rule nations, geographic territories, and entire people groups thus holding them in spiritual bondage. In this section, we will address these high-ranking, territorial demonic powers. It is crucial to distinguish these entities from the demons we cast out of individuals. Although lesser demons may bear the same names as these high-ranking principalities, this alignment merely reflects their connection to these superior entities. In my opinion, the demons, even occult-level demons, are still under the hierarchical structures of these high-ranking, territorial demonic powers.

These top-level, territorial demonic powers operate in the three realms previously discussed: the heavenly realm, the earthly realm, and the underworld. However, as we present these categories and realms to you, it is also important to understand that there are crossovers and interactions between all of these realms.

We are not simply attempting to define demons or territorial demonic powers into a well-defined box, but we are explaining that there are distinctions in these various realms.

The following information about these high-ranking, territorial demonic entities also applies to ground-level, personal deliverance with individuals. You will notice overlapping similarities in their names and characteristics. The traits and functions of these high-ranking territorial entities often carry over into the demons that manifest within individuals. This overlap highlights how these entities influence both broader territories and also, personal spiritual struggles. When leading deliverance sessions for individuals, we will often see demons manifest with the same names as these territorial spirits. However, note that we are simply addressing *a* leviathan, not *the* Leviathan or *a* satan, not *the* Satan. Similarly, we may refer to *a* baal, not *the* Baal. This distinction highlights that we are dealing with lower-ranking demons aligned with, but not equivalent to, these higher-ranking, territorial spirits.

HEAVENLY REALM

Even within these three realms, we find distinct categories in which these high-ranking, territorial demonic powers operate. Understanding these categories helps us discern the level or type of demonic entity that we are dealing with. For example, within the heavenly realm, we can identify specific categories, such as the Queen of Heaven, which are often depicted as a moon goddess or goddess of the sky. Similarly, there is the sun god, often referred to as a King of Heaven. Alongside these, there are other demonic figures often referred to as the Constellations, which are regarded in ancient mythology as their offspring—sons, daughters, or other related entities.

For example, within the Queen of Heaven category, there are numerous deities that manifest in different cultures and times; the same is true of the King of Heaven and the Constellations. This title simply represents a rank or category; depending on the culture, it is expressed through various names and identities. It is crucial to note that some of these names are mentioned in the Bible, while others come from the ancient mythologies, legends, and traditions of different cultures. These entities often morph to operate under new names, expressions, or identities across different regions and cultures.

THE QUEEN OF HEAVEN

Scripture does specifically mention a deity called the Queen of Heaven in Jeremiah 7:18 and four other references in Jeremiah 44. The Hebrew word is *meleket* and simply means "queen."[70] It is distinctive though as the most common Hebrew term for queen is *malkâ*.[71] It is also similar to the form of *melek,* which is translated for the name of the demon, Moloch, as well as the generic usage of king. This will be explored further in the next section.

When we use the term Queen of Heaven, we are using it as a category that includes multiple female, heavenly goddesses that were at the top of the demonic hierarchy. In most cultures, this deity is known as the moon goddess in contrast to a King of Heaven, which would be associated with a male form of the sun god. In further describing this correlation, Rebecca Greenwood states that the Queen of Heaven was associated with the moon god because "it was linked with the cycles of the female body.

Therefore, the moon was the source of blood flow and fertility."[72] Further, Greenwood also states that the Queen of Heaven was at the top of the demonic, hierarchical structure concerning territorial spirits.[73] Some examples of manifestations of the Queen of Heaven include Ishtar, Astarte, Diana, Artemis, Sophia, Cybele, Minerva, Lilith, Jezebel, Venus, Ashtoreth (or Asherah), Isis, Juno, Medusa, Santa Muerte, and Mami Wata.[74]

ASHERAH

Throughout the Old Testament, references to Asherah (also spelled Ashtoreth) are common as a frequent temptation of Israel's worship in the form of idolatry. Ashtoreth, also known as Astarte or Ishtar, was a goddess associated with fertility, love, and war. Worship of Ashtoreth often involved sexual immorality, symbolizing rebellion through the corruption of God's design for purity and holiness in relationships. Solomon's downfall illustrates the devastating consequences of such devotion: "*He* [Solomon] *followed Ashtoreth the goddess of the Sidonians and Molek the detestable god of the Ammonites. So Solomon did evil in the eyes of the Lord; he did not follow the Lord completely, as David his father had done*" (1 Kings 11:5-6 NIV).

Oftentimes, Asherah worship involved a form of a pole or column-like structure with wooden symbols of this female deity. The presence of these poles served as evidence for apostasy and polytheism, which were directly commanded against by God.[75] Further, Asherah is commonly linked with Baal and Baal-worship throughout the Old Testament. Judges 3:7 says, "*So the sons of Israel did what was evil in the sight of the Lord, and they forgot the Lord their God and served the Baals and the Asheroth.*" To worship Asherah is always described as doing evil before the Lord.

In the ancient Canaanite worship system, Baal was viewed as the god who served as king as compared to Yahweh; Asherah was the queen of this system.[76]

In scripture, Ashtoreth and Baal form a spiritual duo of idolatry and immorality. Judges 10:6 (NRSV) records, *"The Israelites again did what was evil in the sight of the Lord, serving the Baals and the Astartes, the gods of Aram, the gods of Sidon, the gods of Moab, the gods of the Ammonites, and the gods of the Philistines. Thus they abandoned the Lord and did not worship him."* The corruption went beyond just individuals as entire families participated in the worship of Asherah. Jeremiah 7:18 (NRSV) records, *"The children gather wood, the fathers kindle fire, and the women knead dough, to make cakes for the queen of heaven, and they pour out drink offerings to other gods, to provoke me to anger."* As referenced here, this "Queen of Heaven" was likely Asherah and led families into rebellion against God.

The Hebrew term for Asherah is twofold: to identify the proper name of this demonic entity when used in singular form and also, to refer to the poles that were used to worship her when used in plural form.[77] In ancient mythology, Asherah is known as the great moon goddess and the mother of the minor gods of the pantheon.[78] Because of the connection to the moon, she was also the goddess of fertility. Much of her worship involved sexual practices. She is also the goddess whom Jezebel worshiped in 1 Kings 18:19: "*Now then, send orders and gather to me all Israel at Mount Carmel, together with 450 prophets of Baal and four hundred prophets of the Asherah, who eat at Jezebel's table.*" This story will be evaluated more in the proceeding section concerning Baal. However, this further reveals this demonic god's hierarchy since Jezebel worshiped her alongside of Baal.

THE KING OF HEAVEN

Following the Queen of Heaven category, another significant category is the King of Heaven, which may also be represented as a sun god. These entities are frequently associated with power, dominance, and rulership within their respective mythologies. "Other sun god names are Ra, Osiris, Horus, Apollo, Zeus, Hercules, Nike, Helios, Dazhbog, Sunna, Mithras, Shamash."[79]

BAAL

Baal was the male demonic deity at the top of the demonic hierarchy and was viewed as the "ruler of the gods."[80] He was the god of many foreign nations that ancient Israel was strictly prohibited from worshiping. Judges 2:11 says, "*Then the sons of Israel did evil in the sight of the Lord and served the Baals.*" His name literally means "lord, owner" in Hebrew.[81] Baal "was a storm god and, as such, the bringer of rain, which in turn, sustained life and made the land fertile."[82] He was also worshiped as a god of fertility. This will be addressed more in the discussion to come about the demon, Mot. Baal was also known as the sun god.[83] The worship of Baal represented a complete turning away from God and His covenant.

An insight into Baal worship is revealed in 1 Kings 18:28: *"So they cried out with a loud voice, and cut themselves according to their custom with swords and lances until blood gushed out on them."* This was right after they had sacrificed an ox to the altar of Baal. From this account, this false demonic god required blood through various rituals including the sacrifice of animals and the blood of the priests.

Let's look further at 1 Kings 17–18 to gain more insights into Baal as well as how these demonic powers interact and function together. At this time, Israel was led by the wicked King Ahab and Queen Jezebel.[84] Jezebel's name "was actually the ritual cry in the worship of Baal."[85] Elijah declared to Ahab in 1 Kings 17:1, "*As the Lord, the God of Israel lives, before whom I stand, there shall certainly be neither dew nor rain during these years, except by my word.*" Elijah then disappeared for the next three years while the drought occurred just as he said it would.

As a prophet, Elijah was the mouthpiece of God to His people. This was not just an idea by the prophet, but this was a direct confrontation against Baal, the god of Ahab and Jezebel, whom Israel was also worshiping at this time. If Baal was truly the god over the rain, then he should have been able to end the drought. Elijah was challenging Baal through this declaration of drought to prove that Yahweh was supreme and ultimately, cause Israel to turn back from their idolatry.

King Ahab puts a decree of death on Elijah's life while he is gone. Jezebel has also been killing off the true prophets of the Lord during this same time.[86] In 1 Kings 18:1, God speaks to Elijah and tells him to return and "Show himself" to Ahab, and God would end the drought. Ahab knew that Elijah was the only one who could actually cause the rain to return, yet he still ordered him to be killed. Why? Ahab had the entire nation deceived that Baal was supreme, not Yahweh. This would reveal the deception and cause Israel to turn away from Baal and back to God. This is why 1 Kings 16:33 describes Ahab as such: "*Ahab did more to provoke the Lord God of Israel to anger than all the kings of Israel who were before him.*"

Elijah calls for a showdown between God and Baal with 450 prophets of Baal and 400 prophets of Asherah who all eat at Jezebel's table while he, by himself, would represent God. He called for this showdown on Mount Carmel before all the nation to witness. God answers by fire while the prophets of Baal and Asherah are made fools of. First Kings 18:39 describes the result of this showdown between God and Baal: "*When all the people saw, they fell on their faces and said, 'The Lord indeed is God; the Lord indeed is God.*'" The nation of Israel was delivered and turned away from their idolatry back to God. Right after this showdown, the drought ends as a heavy rain falls over the land further revealing God's power over all.

MARDUK

Marduk was the head of the ancient Babylonian pantheon.[87] He also was referred to as "the king of the gods."[88] The Hebrew name is *mᵊrōḏaḵ* and literally means, "thy rebellion."[89] This gives further insight into its role as a rebellious principality that was over the wicked enemy of God and its territory, Babylon. Jeremiah 50:2 says, "*Declare and proclaim among the nations. Proclaim it and lift up a flag, do not conceal it. Say, 'Babylon has been captured, Bel has been put to shame, Marduk has been shattered; her idols have been put to shame, her images have been shattered.*'"

Other references to Marduk in scripture are found under the Hebrew name *bel,* which is distinctively different from the previously mentioned false god, Baal.[90] This name is mentioned in Jeremiah 51:44 and Isaiah 46:1. In both cases, the context is judgment against Babylon and her pending fall from power. The prophets, Jeremiah and Isaiah, both declare this fall from glory that was about to come. In the Babylonian creation story, "Marduk is represented as setting the heavenly bodies in order."[91] This deity carried a high rank in the demonic hierarchy and was responsible for the order of the constellations which will be evaluated next.

MARDUK AND THE FREEMASON CURSE

I once had a gentleman with a long history of ministry success come to us for help. Over the years, he had started multiple, thriving ministries, but each one ended in failure as he became trapped in a cycle of sin, confession, demonic torment, and eventual collapse. The torment was so severe that he had attempted suicide multiple times. This cycle had persisted for decades. During a teaching on breaking Masonic curses, he came forward for deliverance. As we began praying, it was revealed that his bloodline carried a curse tied to the Masonic Lodge dating back to the 1700s. The firstborn male on his father's side had been dedicated to the lodge for generations. On his father's deathbed, he had said, "Let the Masonic curse die with me," but still, the curse had continued. The man himself had never joined the Masonic Lodge, yet he lived in torment almost every day of his life. Further prayer revealed that as a baby, his father had taken him into the lodge, pierced his heel, and placed a drop of his blood on the Masonic altar as a dedication to the gods of the lodge.

Once this was uncovered, we led the man in renouncing the specific dedication made by his father and breaking the curse over his life. Almost immediately, a demon manifested calling itself Babel. As I pressed the demon by commanding it to, "Lie not to the Holy Spirit," it revealed its true name, Marduk. Quickly, Marduk revealed its connection to the bloodline curse. After breaking the curse and binding Marduk with its kingdom, we cast it out. Since then, this man's life has been completely transformed. He now runs a successful business, his marriage has been restored, and he lives free of torment! God is faithful!

MOLOCH

Moloch, or Molech, was worshiped through child sacrifice and represents rebellion through the ultimate perversion of worship and life itself. Offering children to Moloch was one of the most heinous practices condemned by God. Leviticus 18:21 (NRSV) declares, "*You shall not give any of your offspring to sacrifice them to Molech and so profane the name of your God: I am the Lord.*" This abhorrent worship practice was often intertwined with Baal worship as seen in Jeremiah's rebuke in Jeremiah 32:35 (NRSV): "*They built the high places of Baal in the valley of the son of Hinnom, to offer up their sons and daughters to Molech, though I did not command them, nor did it enter my mind that they should do this abomination, causing Judah to sin.*" King Josiah's reforms addressed these practices in 2 Kings 23:10 (NRSV). "*He defiled Topheth, which is in the valley of Ben-hinnom, so that no one would make a son or a daughter pass through fire as an offering to Molech.*" The Valley of Ben Hinnom, or Gehenna, became synonymous with hell itself due to these atrocities.

Moloch is described as the god of the Ammonites. First Kings 11:7 describes Solomon's downfall by worshiping this wicked entity: "*Then Solomon built a high place for Chemosh, the abhorrent idol of Moab, on the mountain that is east of Jerusalem, and for Molech, the abhorrent idol of the sons of Ammon.*" The Hebrew word for this demonic entity is *mōleḵ*. It literally means "king."[92] This demonic entity is connected to the false god, Saturn, in Amos 5:26 which will be discussed in the proceeding section.

CONSTELLATIONS

Understanding these categories and their variations across cultures helps provide clarity when addressing spiritual strongholds and their influence in different regions. Second Kings 23:5 mentions further worship to the constellations:

> *Then he* [Josiah] *did away with the idolatrous priests whom the kings of Judah had appointed to burn incense on the high places in the cities of Judah and in the surrounding area of Jerusalem, as well as those who burned incense to Baal, to the sun, to the moon, to the constellations, and to all the remaining heavenly lights* [hosts].

The context to this passage is the reforms implemented by King Josiah after making a new covenant with God on behalf of Israel. This verse addressed Israel's false worship to Baal, the sun, the moon, the constellations, and all the remaining heavenly hosts, referring to all other deities associated with the heavenly realm. The Hebrew term for constellations refers to the cycles of the moon and sun that are utilized in the Zodiac.[93] These were used to help determine time and seasons. However, the address here is against using the Zodiac to source other information—specifically, to predict the fortunes of people or future events.[94] In the modern era, this is the same practice as reading astrological horoscopes. This act is rooted in demonic worship and is a form of idolatry. In this passage, the reference is that not only were these heavenly entities being used to source information, they were also being worshiped as gods.

Astrology and worshiping the constellations is revealed in Jeremiah as a common practice of the other nations. Jeremiah 10:2 says, "*This is what the Lord says: 'Do not learn the way of the nations, and do not be terrified by the signs of the heavens, although the nations are terrified by them.*" In this passage, Israel was impressed by the "signs of the heavens."[95] In Jeremiah 8:2, they are described as actually worshiping these constellations: "*They will spread them out to the sun, the moon, and to all the heavenly lights, which they have loved, which they have served, which they have followed, which they have sought, and which they have worshiped....*" The prophet calls for Israel to repent and turn away from these evil practices and thus, return back to worshiping only God.

Sourcing any information through demonic entities is a dangerous practice that is absolutely prohibited by God. What many fail to recognize in the modern era is that many modern practices in New Age, Wicca, astrology, psychics, mediums, tarot cards, and more utilize this same dangerous practice. When information is sourced through any of these practices, it is sourced through demonic intel, not revelation from God. In scripture, this is often described through the term *divination*. In addition to idolatry through the worship of other gods, God strictly forbids Israel from practicing any form of divination. Leviticus 19:26 says, "*You shall not practice divination nor soothsaying.*" Soothsaying is one of the practices of divination that specifically deals with predicting the future through demonic practices.[96] Jeremiah warns Israel against these demonic practices in Jeremiah 27:9, including, "*Do not to listen to your [false] prophets, your diviners, your dreamers* [interpreters of dreams], *your soothsayers or your sorcerers.*"[97]

Another biblical term that is often used for varying divination practices is *magic*. When most of us hear the word *magic*, we associate it with a show of illusions at a child's birthday party or an entertainment show in Vegas; this is not that. The Hebrew word used in scripture literally means "to practice sorcery."[98] Dr. Joy Vaughn, professor at Asbury Theological Seminary, defines magic as "the management of supernatural powers in such a way that results are virtually guaranteed."[99] Magic involves various practices that often include casting spells or reciting chants. Clearly, all of these forms of divination were prominent within the ancient world but always forbidden for God's people.

DANIEL AND BABYLON

Ancient Babylon was known as the city of sorceries and magic spells according to Isaiah 47:9 and 12. Isaiah 47:13 (ESV) describes the Babylonian astrologers as those who "*divide the heavens, who look at the stars, who make known at the new moons what is coming upon you.*"[100] When King Nebuchadnezzar needed his dream interpreted in Daniel 2:2, he called forth the "wise men" who were listed as magicians, conjurers, sorcerers, and Chaldeans. The implications of this act further reveal how aligned ancient Babylon was with the demonic realm and evil spirits.

To overlay this with the context of Daniel, Daniel was the voice of God in the midst of captivity in a very demonic culture. When the King's "wise men" could not interpret his dream, they respond to the king in Daniel 2:11: "*Moreover, the thing which the king demands is difficult, and there is no one else who could declare it to the king except the gods, whose dwelling place is not with mortal flesh.*" They have summoned and attempted to seek information from the demonic realm but did not succeed; they defend themselves by saying that only gods would have this information. The king orders for all of these men to be put to death. This is what opens the door for Daniel to reveal the one true God who is supreme and has power over *all* other gods by interpreting the dream through Daniel. Daniel 2:27–28 says:

> *Daniel answered before the king and said, "As for the secret about which the king has inquired, neither wise men, sorcerers,*

soothsayer priests, nor diviners are able to declare it to the king. However, there is a God in heaven who reveals secrets, and He has made known to King Nebuchadnezzar what will take place in the latter days. This was your dream and the visions in your mind while on your bed.

Daniel continues in the next several verses to interpret the dream. The king is so pleased with Daniel's interpretation that he responds in Daniel 2:47-48 by giving him a great promotion and many gifts:

The king responded to Daniel and said, "Your God truly is a God of gods and a Lord of kings and a revealer of secrets, since you have been able to reveal this secret." Then the king promoted Daniel and gave him many great gifts, and he made him ruler over the entire province of Babylon, and chief prefect over all the wise men of Babylon.

JESUS AND THE MAGI

The Magi from the east who came to worship Jesus were also considered "wise men." They were not Jewish but were actually Gentiles. Historically, they were proficient in astrology. Matthew 2:1-2 says:

Now after Jesus was born in Bethlehem of Judea in the days of Herod the king, behold, magi from the east arrived in Jerusalem, saying, "Where is He who has been born King of the Jews? For we saw His star in the east and have come to worship Him."

However, the Greek term for "magi" is *magos* and literally means "a sorcerer." It is also the same name given by the Babylonians to describe "the wise men, teachers, priests, physicians, astrologers, seers, interpreters of dreams, augers, soothsayers, sorcerers, etc."[101] These would be the same men described as the "wise men" previously in Daniel 2. This would explain why King Herod responded to this with concern in Matthew 2:3: "*When Herod the king heard this, he was troubled, and all Jerusalem with him.*" Even the Gentiles who worshiped the constellations recognized the birth of Jesus, saw the light of Christ revealed in the sky, and responded with worshiping Him and giving him gifts. This correlates directly to the prophecy of Isaiah in Isaiah 9:2: "*The people who walk in darkness will see a great light; those who live in a dark land, the light will shine on them.*"

SATURN

As a demonic deity, Saturn is mentioned once in scripture in Amos 5:26 (AMP): *"You carried along your king Sikkuth* [sikût] *and Kayyun [your man-made gods of Saturn], your images of your star-god which you made for yourselves [but you brought Me none of the appointed sacrifices]."* Sikkuth was another Babylonian entity which is referred to here as the king; the Hebrew name literally means "the tabernacle of Moloch."[102] Kayyun is also referred to as Kaiwan, Chiun, and Saturn. The Hebrew term literally means "an image or pillar." Therefore, this demonic entity, known as the proper name, Saturn, most likely was represented by the image of the planet, Saturn.[103] In the Babylonian understanding, the name of this deity was also referred to as "The Steady One."[104] The ancient Assyrians were also known to worship Saturn.[105] In the context of Amos 5:26, Sikkuth, Saturn, and even the stars were made in the image of man through idols referring to Israel's apostasy once again.

It is important to note the context and historical timing of Amos's prophecy here. This word went forth on the eve of the Assyrian invasion of Judah, which would ultimately destroy the northern Kingdom of Israel and force them into exile, deported "beyond Damascus."[106] The prophet is asking the people of Judah if they are going to take their false gods and idols with them as God is about to bring judgment upon them for their idolatry. These idols would be useless for them in the coming judgment of God. Amos is also making a contrast that during Israel's time in the wilderness, they did not actively worship God as they should have nor to the extent that they are currently worshiping these false gods of the heavenly realm.

Before his martyrdom, Stephen quotes Amos 5:26-27 in his speech in Acts 7:42-43:

> *But God turned away and gave them over to worship the heavenly lights; as it is written in the book of the prophets: "You did not offer Me victims and sacrifices for forty years in the wilderness, did you, house of Israel? You also took along the tabernacle of Moloch and the star of your god Rompha, the images which you made to worship. I also will deport you beyond Babylon."*

The New Testament recognizes the translation of the proper name, Moloch, while many of the Old Testament translations only mention this name in a footnote. F.F. Bruce explains this quote of Amos by Stephen: "Moloch and Raiphan are members of the 'host of heaven'; Stephen means that the worship of the planetary powers, for which the nation lost its liberty and suffered deportation, was the climax of that idolatrous process which began in the wilderness."[107]

Another important note is that Stephen's quote of Amos changes slightly. Amos 5:27 says, "'*Therefore I will make you go into exile beyond* **Damascus,**' *says the Lord, whose name is the God of armies.*" In Acts 7:43, Stephen changes the location to Babylon. This shift alludes to the same judgment that came upon Jerusalem, the southern kingdom of Israel, later which resulted in the Babylonian captivity; they were worshiping the same false gods as Judah and thus, suffered the same consequences.[108] It is also likely that Stephen used Babylon as he was currently in Jerusalem, the location Israel returned to and rebuilt following the Babylonian exile.

EARTHLY REALM

Spirits of nature, often referred to as nature or elemental spirits, are central to spiritual practices across many belief systems, including Wicca, paganism, shamanism, animism, and various indigenous traditions. These spirits are believed to embody aspects of the natural world such as earth, water, air, fire, plants, and animals. Many traditions categorize them by elements and assign them distinct names and roles.

Earth spirits are often associated with soil, rocks, and caves. Figures like gnomes and dwarfs are believed to protect natural formations and hidden treasures. Water spirits such as mermaids and nymphs are tied to rivers, lakes, and oceans. They are frequently connected with beauty, mystery, and the power of water. Air spirits, like fairies, are connected to the wind and sky, symbolizing freedom and ethereal movement.

In Wicca, these spirits are revered as part of a divine connection to nature and are invoked during rituals for protection, guidance, or harmony. Offerings of flowers, crystals, or food are commonly made to honor and build relationships with these demonic entities. Similarly, shamanic traditions engage with nature spirits as allies or messengers and assist in demonic healings and divination practices.

For example, Native American spirituality includes animal spirits like the eagle and wolf, which represent specific traits and guidance. Celtic spirituality highlights fairies, elves, and banshees that are believed to dwell in forests, hills, and groves and are often tied to the natural cycles and seasons. In Asia, Shinto practitioners worship the *kami*, which are the spirits inhabiting mountains, rivers, and trees. One such example is Mount Fuji's guardian spirit, Konohanasakuya-hime, which is prevalent in Japanese mythology.[109] Hinduism also features river goddesses like Ganga, who personifies the sacred River Ganges, and other spirits that are connected to sacred animals like cows and elephants. Across these traditions, nature spirits are seen as the guardians of balance in the earth and are approached with deep reverence and worship.

WILDERNESS

A specific location in the earthly realm that needs to be understood through the ancient worldview is the wilderness, the place where Israel wandered for forty years after their Exodus from Egypt. In the ancient worldview, the wilderness was closely associated with darkness and viewed as a habitation for hostile demon-gods and evil spirits.[110] Many demonic entities that are associated with the wilderness are translated as natural creatures or animals which ultimately lose their spiritual understanding and context. The desert wilderness was a place of sinister evil which cannot be overemphasized. Many of the demonic creatures and entities that resided there were discussed in phantom-like terminology and caused great fear of this physical location. Heiser states that these creatures were commonly called "desert-demons."[111]

AZAZEL

The first hostile deity worth mentioning specifically from the wilderness is Azazel. Leviticus 16–17 and the scapegoat used in the Day of Atonement ceremony provide the backdrop to the ancient understanding of this demon. Azazel is the proper name of a demonic deity. The Dead Sea Scrolls and the book of Enoch provide additional background to this demon stating that he was the leader of the rebellious spiritual beings of Genesis 6 and was connected to the god of death and the underworld in many Ugaritic texts.[112] Further, Azazel was known to have resided in the desert as a place associated with supernatural evil and outside of holy ground.[113] Many modern English translations, including the NIV, NASB, and KJV, use the term "scapegoat" or "the goat that goes away" rather than the proper title of Azazel. Leviticus 16:8-10 indicates a parallel that supports the translation of the proper name versus "scapegoat," as it states that one goat was sacrificed to the proper name, Yahweh, while the other goat was for Azazel, another proper name:

> *Aaron shall cast lots for the two goats, one lot for the Lord and the other lot for the scapegoat* [Azazel]. *Then Aaron shall offer the goat on which the lot for the Lord fell, and make it a sin offering. But the goat on which the lot for the scapegoat* [Azazel] *fell shall be presented alive before the Lord, to make*

atonement upon it, to send it into the wilderness as the scapegoat [Azazel].

Concerning the Atonement sacrifice and the goat for Azazel, it is crucial to note that Israel did not sacrifice a goat to a demonic deity as this would violate their covenant with God and be an act of idolatry; this was also not a ransom nor a debt that was owed. The goat that was sacrificed for Yahweh purged the sins and impurities for the entire nation of Israel and purified the sanctuary.[114] Those sins were symbolically placed upon the goat for Azazel, and it was sent outside the realm of Israel. Heiser describes this as such: "Sin had to be 'transported' to where evil belonged—the territory outside Israel, under the control of gods set over the pagan nations… Azazel was getting what belonged to him: sin."[115] Though the sins of the nation were sent out of Israel's camp and into the wilderness, the goat for Azazel was simply returning back to the evil place where it came from.

Azazel is also a demon that we encounter often during ground-level deliverance with individuals. This is a demon that typically is near the top of a demonic kingdom, and is often associated with Satanism or ritualistic practices that offer blood. This is a demon that craves blood and rarely comes to a ritual unless it is first offered animal blood or the blood of humans. I actually have in my possession an instrument similar to a throat-hook; it is a type of knife that was used in multiple generations from a specific family that offered blood sacrifices to this particular demon.

LILITH

Another evil deity worth mentioning specifically is the Mesopotamian wind-goddess, Lilith.[116] This nocturnal demon resided with other haunted monsters of the desert including birds, snakes, jackals, wolves, and goats. Isaiah 34:14 describes this demonic entity in the wilderness among other demonic creatures: "*The desert creatures will meet with the wolves, the goat also will cry to its kind. Yes, the night-bird* [Lilith] *will settle there and will find herself a resting place.*" Lilith is translated as "night-bird" (NASB), "night creature" (NIV), and "screech owl" (KJV). The New Revised Standard Version is the only modern translation to use the proper name, Lilith. These other translations denote a common animal that is neutral; it simply does not due justice or proper context to the ancient understanding of this evil demon.

It is not uncommon to encounter Lilith as a high-level, territorial spirit ruling over specific regions. Additionally, this demon is frequently summoned by occult practitioners. For those transitioning from "white" witchcraft to the "dark" side of witchcraft, Lilith is often one of the primary entities invoked during rituals. As one of the chief spirits in hierarchical demonic structures, Lilith frequently appears in individuals who are demonized. Our teams and I have encountered and dealt with this demon numerous times in deliverance sessions.

Lilith has become increasingly popular due to her appearance as a lead role in the video game, Diablo, which means "devil" in Spanish. In 2023, as a part of the launch of Diablo 4, Kentucky Fried Kitchen (KFC) joined up with Diablo to support their launch efforts. They made a reward for purchasing KFC food that, in turn, gave special perks in the game. Further, their mass marketing featured the image of Lilith. Their cups were printed with the phrase "Lilith welcomes all." Many have been desensitized by the wickedness of this demon, making her appear only as a desirable character in a video game. This is a common scheme of the enemy which is evidenced in much of the entertainment world.

LEVIATHAN

Leviathan is described in scripture as a sea serpent, sea monster, or sea dragon. Regardless of its physical description, Leviathan is always connected to water and the marine world in the earthly realm. There are many references in scripture of this ancient sea-serpent. Isaiah 27:1 says in the context of blessing Israel, "*On that day the Lord will punish Leviathan the fleeing serpent, With His fierce and great and mighty sword, Even Leviathan the twisted serpent; And He will kill the dragon who lives in the sea.*" Job 41 gives extensive descriptions of Leviathan, specifically in verses 33-34: "*Nothing on earth is like him, one made without fear. He looks on everything that is high; he is king over all the sons of pride.*"

Psalm 74:14 gives a further description describing Leviathan as having multiple heads: "*You crushed the heads of Leviathan; You gave him as food for the creatures of the wilderness.*" In many ancient Eastern cultures, demons are actively worshiped through statues that appear like a multi-headed serpent entity that could be a form of Leviathan based on these biblical descriptions. While in Cambodia recently, I noticed a prominent demon worshiped through statues and idols known as Shesha Naga. This multi-headed serpent was often found at entrances to sacred temples and worship sites, including Ankor Wat, the largest religious structure in the world.

Leviathan was known as a creature of chaos. While not always named specifically in scripture, there are other references that are associated with this demon. It is important to note here that the sea was a symbol of chaos in the ancient worldview. Hebrew wisdom literature, especially the Psalms, frequently deal with the struggle between God and His created order within the earth against the evil forces of chaos that are actively trying to disrupt this order.[117] God gives the sea its boundaries (Genesis 1:6-7), even though the sea continually attempts to push those limits as far as it can. This is the domain of Leviathan. This demon will push the limits to challenge boundaries and cause great chaos and confusion in both the earth and also in the lives of those who have been influenced by it.

More about this demon is revealed in Psalm 8; this is a creation psalm that describes God's created order as well as humanity's authority within creation. Psalm 8:6-8 further details the authority of mankind: "*You have him rule over the works of Your hands; You have put everything under his feet, all sheep and oxen, and also the animals of the field, the birds of the sky, and the fish of the sea, whatever passes through the paths of the seas.*" Genesis 1:26 describes this same authority given by God to Adam, specifically to "*rule over the fish of the sea and over the birds of the sky.*" The phrase, "*whatever passes through the paths of the seas*" though is referencing more than just the fish and natural marine world. This phrase correlates directly with Psalm 104 and Job 38:11, 41:10-11, and 33; all of these passages directly reference Leviathan by name. In context, then, the psalmist is also indirectly referencing Leviathan in Psalm 8:8 and thus, man's authority over this demonic entity in the earthly realm. This also furthers humanity's assignment to bring godly order into the chaos of the earth.

In ground-level warfare, it is fairly common to see Leviathan manifest in people's lives, as oftentimes, revealing itself initially as the demon of pride. Pride, a lower-ranking demon in the category of sin, may present itself first, but when pressed, it will frequently reveal its true nature as Leviathan. When Leviathan is present, individuals often feel convinced that they are right, and everyone else is wrong. This demon twists words and perceptions and distorts the truth in order to isolate people and cut them off from godly relationships. In its strategic attacks, Leviathan often works to build individuals up in pride, isolating them emotionally or spiritually, which then creates fertile ground for other demons to enter and further dismantle their lives. This makes it a particularly insidious spirit to confront and cast out and thus, requires discernment and perseverance.

BEHEMOTH

Behemoth is paralleled with Leviathan in Job 40 as the land creature of chaos. He is a beast-like creature described as having supernatural strength with references to the "*power in the muscles of his belly,*" "*His bones are tubes of bronze,*" and "*His limbs are like bars of iron*" (Job 40:16,18). This chapter also describes that he is confident and fears nothing. He is served by various elements of nature, and according to Job 40:21-22, he is described to reside under and be protected by the lotus plants: "*He lies down under the lotus plants, in the hiding place of the reeds and the marsh. The lotus plants cover him with shade; the willows of the brook surround him.*"

While in Cambodia recently, I noticed how common the lotus flower was depicted in conjunction with Buddhism and Hinduism. In the practice of yoga, one of the meditation poses is called "the lotus." Another belief is that the lotus flower is a symbol of purity, good luck, and prosperity. Buddhists believe that Buddha reached full transcendence as he rose out of the impurities of the flesh into the state of purity attained only in the divine realm.

As a result, many Buddhas are depicted as being supported by lotus flowers "emphasizing their transcendence connection to the divine."[118] In Hinduism, the female deity, Lakshmi, is known as the goddess of prosperity. She is depicted with four arms adorned with lotus petals and coming out of a large lotus flower as she is believed to have been born out of it.[119] Similarly to Buddhist beliefs, the Hindu belief symbolizes the lotus flower with purity and ascension out of the muddy, material world and into the divine, pure nature just as a lotus plant that naturally grows out of the mud and in extreme conditions into a beautiful flower.

I want to share a story of how God uses divine revelation to provide spiritual intelligence for deliverance ministry and strategic-level warfare. During this same trip to Cambodia, God had just revealed to me these specific scriptures about Behemoth and how this demon appeared to be overlooked in deliverance when compared to Leviathan. It was as if this entity was trying to remain hidden in order to not be discovered behind areas of chaos and destruction. I continued to pray and document what the Lord was revealing to me.

Just a few days later, we were visiting a remote mountain that contains the world's largest reclining Buddha as well as tens of thousands of other idols and statues spread out over multiple worship sites. This location was one of the most demonic places that I have ever personally visited as the worship of these demonic entities was almost overwhelming. While going up to a large statue of the Hindu god of war, Shiva, we removed our shoes at the base of this worship site as required. We prayer walked around the statue and declared the Kingdom of God to come to this demonic mountain, topple these idols, and deliver all of those who make the pilgrimage to worship here. Upon returning to our shoes, Mike found a single lotus flower placed specifically inside his shoe. This confirmed that God was speaking to me about Behemoth as Job 40:21-22 is the only mention in all of scripture of a lotus plant. During this time, we also started receiving several other messages from other deliverance ministers who were dealing with Behemoth in individual sessions for the first time. This became specific spiritual intelligence that God was delivering both His people and also, specific territories from this demonic entity.

BELIAL

A third proper name worth mentioning from scripture is Belial. In ancient understanding, Belial was associated with the most heinous crimes against God or Israel's religious order.[120] Belial is mentioned in the Old Testament 26 times and once in the New Testament. Out of the 26 Old Testament references, 16 are connected directly with David in 1 and 2 Samuel and the psalms; more than half of these usages reveal that David was directly engaged in a battle with this demonic power during his life.

Belial is also revealed in the life of Eli the priest. In 1 Samuel 1, Eli sees Hannah weeping at the temple of the Lord over her inability to conceive a child. Eli assumes she is drunk and accuses her of being a "worthless woman." The Hebrew translation for "worthless woman" is actually a "daughter of Belial." Eli described a righteous woman's prayers before the Lord as demonic. In 1 Samuel 2, a contrast is made between Eli's family and Samuel's family revealing the sinfulness of Eli's sons and the righteousness of Samuel's family.[121] Ironically, in 1 Samuel 2:12, Eli's sons are described as "worthless men." The Hebrew translation is "the sons of Belial." Verses 12-17 (NASB95) describe their sins and just how wicked they were:

> *Now the sons of Eli were* worthless men [the sons of Belial]; *they did not know the Lord and the custom of the priests with the people. When any man was offering a sacrifice, the priest's servant would come while the meat was boiling, with a three-pronged fork in his hand. Then he would thrust it into the pan, or kettle, or caldron, or pot; all that the fork brought up the priest would take for himself. Thus they did in Shiloh to all the Israelites who came there. Also, before they burned the fat, the priest's servant would come and say to the man who was sacrificing, "Give the priest meat for roasting, as he will not take boiled meat from you, only raw." If the man said to him, "They must surely burn the fat first, and then take as much as you desire," then he would say, "No, but you shall give it to me now; and if not, I will take it by force." Thus the sin of the young men was very great before the Lord, for the men despised the offering of the Lord.*

Sadly, Eli did not even recognize the true righteousness of the Lord when it was on display right in front of him through Hannah. Instead, he was deceived by the evil hearts of his own children. This proper translation drastically changes the understanding of this narrative: the sons of Eli were not just "worthless scoundrels" as translated by most modern translations, but they were influenced by a demonic power that corrupted the entire priesthood of God; this caused the priests to sin by defiling the sacred offerings made by the nation of Israel to God. Further, 1 Samuel 2:22 states that they were also having sexual relations with women who were serving at the doorway to the Tent of Meeting, the place that housed God's presence. This is the direct result of demonic influence which affected the entire nation of Israel. It was not just Eli's sons that needed deliverance but also the nation of Israel. Another observation can be made from this story: Belial targets the priests and desires to defile and corrupt not only them, but also the religious structures and acts of worship to God.

Paul specifically addresses Belial by name in 2 Corinthians 6:14-15: *"Do not be mismatched* [unequally yoked] *with unbelievers; for what do righteousness and lawlessness share together, or what does light have in common with darkness? Or what harmony does Christ have with Belial, or what does a believer share with an unbeliever?"* Some translations use the generic term satan, but in the Greek, this is the proper name of the demon, Belial. In summary, Belial consistently represents worthlessness, lawlessness, and malice throughout all of scripture. These characteristics are important insights and spiritual intelligence for both deliverance and strategic-level warfare.

JEZEBEL

In the Old Testament, Jezebel was a historical figure and queen who married King Ahab. Much can be learned through the story of Elijah about this figure and just how evil she was. From the previous discussion of Jezebel, we can observe that she targets the prophets of God and desires to silence them by killing them. First Kings 18:13 says, "*Has it not been reported to my master what I did when Jezebel killed the prophets of the Lord.*" After the showdown, 1 Kings 19:2 records Jezebel making a threat to kill Elijah which causes him to flee and hide: "*Then Jezebel sent a messenger to Elijah, saying, 'So may* ***the gods*** *do to me and more so, if by about this time tomorrow I do not make your life like the life* [soul like the soul] *of one* *of them.*'" Let me point out here that "the gods" referenced are the *elohim*. This further reveals the demonic hierarchy that Jezebel was submitted to these principalities that she promised to kill Elijah to appease them.

In 1 Kings 21, following this threat to Elijah and his time in the cave, Jezebel makes another promise, but this time to her husband, Ahab. She promises to get him the vineyard beside their palace that was owned by Naboth. She devises a plot against Naboth and writes letters under Ahab's name declaring, "*Proclaim a fast and seat Naboth at the head of the people; and seat* ***two worthless men*** *before him, and let them testify against him, saying, 'You cursed God and the king.' Then take him out and stone him to death*" (1 Kings 21:9-10 NASB95). In Hebrew, "two worthless men" are literally "two sons of Belial." In this entire story, evil powers are working together against the people of God and his prophet. Jezebel did not act alone: the sons of Belial did her dirty work at her command. In deliverance ministry, the same concept is true. Demons function together to strengthen their influence over an individual or a region. In this story, Jezebel was submitted to the *elohim*, which included Baal and Asherah, but still had power over Belial as they acted as her minions on her behalf.

In the New Testament, Jezebel is listed as a spiritual entity in Revelation 2:20-23 who has seduced the church at Thyatira:

> *But I have this against you, that you tolerate the woman Jezebel, who calls herself a prophetess, and she teaches and leads My bond-servants astray so that they commit sexual immorality and eat things sacrificed to idols. I gave her time to repent, and she does not want to repent of her sexual immorality. Behold, I will throw her on a bed of sickness, and those*

who commit adultery with her into great tribulation, unless they repent of her deeds. And I will kill her children with plague, and all the churches will know that I am He who searches the minds and hearts; and I will give to each one of you according to your deeds.

This description reveals a kind of spirit that is characteristic of the natural, historical person. When Jezebel manifests, it is not the actual person but the spirit as described in Revelation.

Characteristics of Jezebel from both of these passages are helpful for spiritual intelligence. Jezebel desires absolute control and power ensuring she rules as queen. She manipulates to gain this control through seduction and sexual immorality. Further, she demands worship of the same gods that she worships through deception. While she has a level of power in the demonic hierarchy, she can also be submissive to other demonic entities. She strategically targets the prophetic voice of God and those who operate in it; her desire is silence through death. Ahab was a weak king; Jezebel seeks power and influence by preying on those who are weak, seducing them to enter into relationship and covenant with her, and ultimately, controlling them, their actions, and their influence. She is wicked and will do whatever necessary to carry out her desires and agenda.

THE UNDERWORLD

The demons of the underworld are often personified by dark, skeletal images of death. There are a range of demonic deities across all cultures including Baron Samedi, Santa Muerte, Anubis, Thanatos (Greek), Hel (Norse), Mot (Canaanite), Morrigan (Celtic), Shinigami (Japanese), Santa Muerte (Mexican), Ankou

(Breton), Mictlantecuhtli (Aztec), Samhain spirits (Celtic), Baron Samedi (Haitian Voodoo), Yama (Hindu/Buddhist), Kali (Hindu), Ghede (Haitian Voodoo), Hades (Greek), Pluto (Roman), and many more.

HADES

A New Testament scripture that needs to be evaluated through the same ancient cosmology and with the awareness of modern translations is Matthew 16:13-20. The reference to the rock was a physical location that Jesus was standing on at that moment located at Caesarea Philippi, at the foot of Mount Hermon.[122] In the early first century, this same location was also called "Panias" as it served as the worship center for the demonic deity of Pan.[123] In the Old Testament, this same location served as an idolatrous worship hub under King Jeroboam[124] as well as a Canaanite worship center for Baal.[125] Jesus, as well as those present for this encounter, would have been familiar with both the past and current contexts of this location as well as the understanding that it had been a sacrificial worship center for many demonic deities for thousands of years. The supernatural understanding of this location cannot be quickly dismissed or overlooked.

The King James Version famously translates verse 18 to say, "*The gates of hell will not prevail against it.*" Much of the modern church has widely accepted this translation by implying that "hell," as a place of eternal torment or damnation, will not be able to stand against the church and her salvation in Jesus. Some have placed this passage within a message that every power of hell can wage war against the church without limits, but as long as believers just "hold on" until Jesus returns, they will eventually be saved. This interpretation alludes to a powerless church just barely existing and struggling to win the cosmic war between the demonic realm and the earthly realm. It also implies that the church is only on the defensive side of this cosmic battle, just waiting for enemy attacks, and not progressing forward in an offensive posture.

A further problem with this translation is that the word "hell" is not actually used, but instead, the proper name, "Hades." In ancient cosmology, Hades was known as the god of the underworld and the lord of the dead.[126] In essence, "hell" could be considered the evil domain of the underworld, but this was a confrontational challenge by Jesus to a specific, named entity: Hades, the one over that evil world. Heiser states that in this verse, "Jesus challenges the authority of the Lord of the dead."[127] This was a declaration of war by Jesus in order to lead the nation into deliverance and freedom.

Another theological key to further understand what Jesus said in this declaration is to recognize that it is the *gates* of Hades that will not prevail. Gates are not offensive weapons but are defensive structures.[128] In ancient Israel, gates served as the single most important element of defense against attacking enemy forces as they were located within the exterior walls of the city, granting or closing access.[129] The prophet Jeremiah described a terrifying reality of a city "that has no gates or bars."[130] Isaiah further adds that a city is strong only when it is able to "turn back the battle at the gate."[131] In this context, then, the gates of the underworld are no match for the advancing Kingdom of God through the declaration of war from Jesus. Their gates will ultimately fail.

Thus, in this cosmological worldview, "The kingdom of God is the aggressor."[132] This drastically shifts the understanding that the church is just anxiously awaiting the next demonic attack from the enemy in a purely defensive posture, but instead, the church is now on the front lines launching an assault by the words of Jesus against every demonic structure and physical location controlled by evil. Every demonic deity and hostile god is now under attack and will not prevail. Every realm in the ancient cosmological structure is now involved and actively engaged in this battle.

MOT/DEATH

Mot was an ancient Canaanite god that sometimes is referenced also as Motu.[133] He was known as the god of death and was believed to reside in the underworld. He is associated with the extreme summer heat and arid climate of the desert that made it hard to grow and produce crops. The ancient belief was that Mot was an ongoing enemy of Baal. Baal was believed to be the god that made it rain which ended droughts and caused the harvest to produce. It is easy to see how these two demonic forces were constantly battling in the natural realm of the desert climate, between rain and drought, literally, between life and death. The legend of Mot states that this false god battled Baal and defeated him. Baal is forced to descend into the underworld and is reported as dead. A female demonic deity, Anat, goes searching for Baal and launches an attack on Mot in the underworld. Baal is revived and taken back to his realm; this caused the hostility and continual battle between Mot and Baal, the underworld, and the heavenly realm.[134]

Let's briefly look at the life of David and how he encountered Mot. David was described as a man of war in scripture who faced and defeated a multitude of enemies throughout his life.[135] The tendency is to focus on the natural enemies he defeated, which include the lion, the bear,[136] and Goliath, the Philistine giant.[137] After all of the great military victories in his life, David writes a psalm of deliverance which is recorded in 2 Samuel 22.

> *And David spoke the words of this song to the Lord in the day that the Lord delivered him from the hand of all his enemies and from the hand of Saul. He said, "The Lord is my rock and my fortress and my deliverer; My God, my rock, in whom I take refuge, My shield and the horn of my salvation, my stronghold and my refuge; My savior, You save me from violence. I call upon the Lord, who is worthy to be praised, And I am saved from my enemies"* (2 Samuel 22:1-4 NASB95).

This is the song of deliverance and victory by David who was worshiping God for delivering him from *all* of his enemies. However, what if David was not just speaking of natural enemies but also spiritual enemies that he had defeated throughout his life? Before this psalm, David contrasts two specific groups: all his enemies and the hand of Saul. In ancient Hebrew writing, especially in the Psalms, parallelism is a common writing technique used in poetry. The contrast here is between Saul, his natural enemy, and all of his enemies, his spiritual enemies. This case is strengthened by the next few verses of this psalm:

> *For the waves of death encompassed me;*
> *The torrents of destruction overwhelmed me;*
> *The cords of Sheol surrounded me;*
> *The snares of death confronted me* (2 Samuel 22:5-6).

In verse 5, David uses parallelism to contrast "the waves of death" and "the torrents of destruction" and how both greatly affected him. "Destruction" is actually the Hebrew name, *Belial*. "Death" is a form of the Hebrew name, Mot, the god of death.[138] In verse 6, Sheol is the proper name of the underworld, which was the land of the dead, the location of chaos, and the source of all forms of evil demons. "Death" in verse 6 is the same form as in verse 5. Following this pattern of parallelism, using the proper names, these verses could also be written as such:

> For the waves of Mot encompassed me;
> The torrents of Belial overwhelmed me;
> The cords of Sheol surrounded me;
> The snares of Mot confronted me.

This psalm of deliverance was the victory song of David over *all* of these evil demons at the end of his life! God was faithful to David and will also be faithful to us.

One observation made by Dr. Michael Heiser is that for ancient Israel, "Anything that threatened death might be associated with the realm of the dead and the disembodied spirits therein."[139] As we discuss these next passages, this observation will help provide a framework. The prophet Hosea makes another correlation between Death and Sheol as proper names in Hosea 13:14: "*Shall I ransom them from the power of Sheol? Shall I redeem them from death? O Death, where are your thorns? O Sheol, where is your sting? Compassion will be hidden from My sight.*" This is the same form of the Hebrew word for death as used in 2 Samuel 22:5-6. However, in Hosea, Death is personified and translated as a proper name which should read as the proper name, Mot.

Another passage where Death is personified and could be read as the proper name of Mot is Job 18:13-14 (NASB95): *"His skin is devoured by disease, the firstborn of death devours his limbs. He is torn from the security of his tent, and they march him before the king of terrors."*[140] The context of this passage is an address to a wicked man in a generic sense. Disease is described as Death's first son. Often, scripture says, "the terror of the king" or "the terror of the kingdom." It is inverted here, implying a specific name that is referred to as "the king of terrors." In the Hebrew, melek̲ is literally "the king," but also the proper name of the demon, Moloch. In Amos 5:26, the "king" that Israel worshiped instead of God was Moloch; it is the same name in both places.[141] See the previous section for more information on Moloch.

Scripture often describes death as when someone has "come under" death in a literal sense; the implication is that the influence of Mot is literal death. This is important to note for deliverance ministry. Hosea 13:1 could literally be translated then, as "*He incurred guilt with regard to Baal and **came under Mot**.*"[142] The result of "coming under Mot" is literal death. In contrast, Isaiah 25:8 says, "*He* [God] *will swallow up **death** for all time.*" God will ultimately "swallow up death" which is the same translation that could be read "God will swallow up Mot," thus revoking his power and influence.[143]

In the New Testament, Paul quotes Isaiah 25:8 in 1 Corinthians 15:54, now stating that "*Death has been swallowed up in victory.*" Once again, Death is capitalized here implying a proper name. In the very next verse, 1 Corinthians 15:55, Paul quotes Hosea 13:14: "*Where, O Death, is your victory? Where, O Death, is your sting?*" Again, Death is capitalized implying the proper name of Mot. Paul's reference is that in the context of the New Covenant and through the resurrection of Jesus, He has conquered *all* of these demonic entities and given us the power to conquer them all! Christians are promised deliverance and the overcoming power over *all* demons, even the false god of Death.

BIBLICAL AND OTHER DEMONIC TRINITIES

Over many years of deliverance ministry, I have studied the trio of Baal, Asherah (Ashtoreth or Astarte), and Moloch (or Molech), prominent pagan deities that the Israelites were repeatedly warned against worshiping. These deities can be understood as a demonic counterfeit trinity and symbolize rebellion against God through idolatry, immorality, and child sacrifice. Each one represents a perversion of God's character and His purposes for humanity, further showcasing the enemy's plan to corrupt worship, purity, and all forms of life itself.

While I will be referencing the demonic trinity of Baal, Asherah, and Moloch, it is important to understand that this is simply a representative example. In deliverance ministry, I have often observed the formation of a "demonic trinity" by various combinations of demons. For instance, I have seen Zeus, Persephone, and Leviathan operating together as well as Poseidon, Lilith, and Python. The key point is that whether you are ministering to individuals or discerning the territorial demonic spirits of a region, it is common to encounter three spirits working in collaboration to maintain their stronghold. For example, if you identify Asherah in a person, you should also search for Baal and Moloch, as they often operate together. Similarly, if you find a "queen" spirit, you should look for a "king" spirit and another spirit that functions in alignment with them. This pattern can also be seen in false familial spirits. If you uncover a false father or mother spirit, be attentive to the possibility of a third spirit working alongside them.

Recognizing these collaborative, demonic structures is critical for breaking their influence thoroughly and effectively.

Specifically, these three entities—Baal, Asherah, and Moloch—reflect Satan's counterfeit of the Holy Trinity. Baal, the counterfeit father, represents pride and rebellion and lures people into worshiping power and prosperity. Asherah, the counterfeit spirit, corrupts purity through immorality and perverts God's design for relationships. Moloch, the counterfeit sacrifice, demands destruction and death thus perverting worship through human sacrifice. Together, this unholy trinity reveals Satan's strategy to keep family bloodlines and territories in bondage. By understanding the influence of these entities in Scripture, we gain valuable insights into how their schemes continue to operate even today, often disguised under different names.

When people understand that they are fighting for more than just their own freedom and realize that they are contending for their family's freedom and even for others in their region, they gain a deeper revelation of the seriousness of deliverance. Recognizing someone as a first-generation Curse Breaker compels us to be exceptionally thorough in the process. It also underscores the importance of noting and recording the spiritual intelligence revealed during the session. Deliverance ministry is not just about addressing the immediate; it is about laying a foundation for transformation that extends through bloodlines and territories.

CHAPTER 6

DEMON KINDS AND CATEGORIES

In Mark 9:14-29, we encounter a powerful story that sheds light on deliverance ministry and the spiritual dynamics of the demonic realm:

> *When they came to the other disciples, they saw a large crowd around them and the teachers of the law arguing with them. As soon as all the people saw Jesus, they were overwhelmed with wonder and ran to greet him. "What are you arguing with them about?" he asked. A man in the crowd answered, "Teacher, I brought you my son, who is possessed by a spirit that has robbed him of speech. Whenever it seizes him, it throws him to the ground. He foams at the mouth, gnashes his teeth and becomes rigid. I asked your disciples to drive out the spirit, but they could not."*
>
> *"You unbelieving generation," Jesus replied, "how long shall I stay with you? How long shall I put up with you? Bring the boy to me." So they brought him. When the spirit saw Jesus, it immediately threw the boy into a convulsion. He fell to the ground and rolled around, foaming at the mouth. Jesus asked the boy's father, "How long has he been like this?" "From childhood," he answered. "It has often thrown him into fire or water to kill him. But if you can do anything, take pity on us and help us." "If you can?" said Jesus. "Everything is possible for one who believes."*

Immediately the boy's father exclaimed, "I do believe; help me overcome my unbelief!" When Jesus saw that a crowd was running to the scene, he rebuked the impure spirit. "You deaf and mute spirit," he said, "I command you, come out of him and never enter him again." The spirit shrieked, convulsed him violently and came out. The boy looked so much like a corpse that many said, "He's dead." But Jesus took him by the hand and lifted him to his feet, and he stood up. After Jesus had gone indoors, his disciples asked him privately, "Why couldn't we drive it out?" He replied, "This kind can come out only by prayer" (Mark 9:14–29 NIV).

This passage offers critical insights into the nature of deliverance. The man tells Jesus, "I brought my son to Your disciples for them to cast the demon out of him, but they could not." The disciples had successfully delivered people from demons before, so what was different this time? Jesus answers in verse 29, explaining, "*This kind can come out only by prayer.*"

Many people focus solely on the prayer aspect, but I want to draw your attention to the phrase "this kind." The Greek word used here is *genos*[144] and means "a group that is distinct or different from another group." Jesus is giving us insights into the demonic realm by further indicating that there are different "kinds" or "types" of evil spirits with unique characteristics and power. This particular demon was of a kind that the disciples had not encountered before, which is why they were unable to cast it out. This story also highlights an essential principle for deliverance ministry: there are different types and levels of evil spirits. Understanding this principle is crucial for effectively setting people free. Jesus, while rebuking His disciples, was also revealing a deeper reality: not all demons operate the same way. There are varying kinds and levels of demonic power, each requiring discernment and preparation. To expand on this concept, let's examine Matthew 12:43-45 (NIV):

> *When an impure spirit comes out of a person, it goes through arid places seeking rest and does not find it. Then it says, "I will return to the house I left." When it arrives, it finds the house unoccupied, swept clean and put in order. Then it goes and takes with it seven other spirits more wicked than itself, and they go in and live there. And the final condition of that person is worse than the first. That is how it will be with this wicked generation.*

This passage reveals significant insights into the nature and behavior of demons. First, the impure spirit "seeks rest" suggesting it becomes tired or weakened. This challenges the notion that spiritual beings are tireless; instead, this passage shows that even demons experience fatigue. The demon, being self-aware, says to itself, "I will return to the house I left." This reveals a level of intelligence and intentionality. Moreover, it communicates with seven other spirits that indicates a coordinated strategy to further demonize the individual. These spirits are described as "more wicked" than the original demon, thus revealing that there are levels of wickedness among demons.

This passage supports the idea that demons operate within a hierarchical structure. The original demon may have had the legal right to the person, but when it began losing control, it sought reinforcements: spirits of greater strength or wickedness. While this is not explicitly stated, the text suggests a form of spiritual scheming: the demon, recognizing its weakness, invites stronger spirits to secure its hold over the individual.

In both passages, we see evidence of the varying kinds and ranks of demons, from *genos* in Mark 9 to "levels of wickedness" in Matthew 12. These biblical accounts align with our experiences in deliverance ministry where some demons clearly exhibit a higher degree of power or authority than others. Understanding the existence of different kinds, levels, and hierarchies of demons equips us to approach deliverance ministry with greater wisdom and effectiveness. Further, it reminds us that, just like the disciples in Mark 9, we must rely on prayer, discernment, and the leading of the Holy Spirit to address the unique challenges of each deliverance.

HOW DEMONS GET IN MAY NOT BE HOW THEY MANIFEST

As we explore demonization, it is crucial to understand that the entry point, referring to what allows a demon to gain access, is often distinct from how it manifests in a person's life. Typically, how a demon manifests is referred to as the presenting issue. Oftentimes, this is connected to the stronghold that the demon constructs after gaining entry through a legal right. Think of the entry point as the front door of a house and the stronghold as the house itself. Once a demon gains access, it begins constructing a "house" within the person: a structure made up of thoughts and emotions tied to those ways of thinking. The presenting issue, such as sexual addiction, drug addiction, anger, violence, etc. is the outward symptom of this internal structure. These manifestations result from the stronghold of thinking and emotions that the demon has built within the person's psyche: specifically their mind, will, and emotions, or what we call "the soul."

When we discuss different types of demons, you will begin to see how this process operates in greater detail. For now, though, understand that the legal right opens the door for a demon to enter, and the stronghold is what allows the demon to maintain its presence in a person's life. The demon draws its strength from the stronghold which thrives on the person's agreement with the demon's agenda. If the person continues yielding to sin and temptation, the stronghold grows even stronger within their thinking and emotions thus giving the demon more power.

For example, consider a person who, at 12 years old, participated in a séance while using a Ouija board and communicated with a demon. This single event could serve as the legal point of entry for demonization, even if they never participated in witchcraft or occult practices again. Once inside, the demon might build a stronghold of lust and perversion that is rooted in an addiction to pornography. This stronghold can mask the original legal point of entry and make it easier to focus on the presenting issue while neglecting the root cause. Many spend time addressing the stronghold without first removing the legal right.

Let me share Laura's story with you. Laura joined one of our semi-private group deliverance sessions. During the interview process, she spoke about the stronghold of homosexuality that she faced in her relationships. She felt broken and deeply desired freedom from the struggles she carried within. As the deliverance minister worked with her, Laura frequently redirected the conversation to her sexual struggles. However, the minister's experience led her to dig deeper as she sought to uncover the root cause: the legal right of entry for the spiritual bondage she was experiencing.

Through prayer and compassionate questioning, Laura began to share about her family history. It was revealed that her grandfather had been involved in Freemasonry as a high-ranking member; this is a connection often associated with generational curses of death and destruction. Additionally, Laura disclosed that her grandfather had molested her in her childhood. These revelations helped identify the source of the spiritual oppression. During the deliverance process, after a brief interrogation of the demons, it was discovered that Jezebel was connected to the molestation, and Lucifer was connected to the Freemasons. Through renouncing the ties to Freemasonry and releasing forgiveness for past hurts from her trauma, Laura experienced a profound breakthrough. The legal rights we removed and the demons that had affected her life were cast out in Jesus's name!

What stands out in Laura's testimony is that she initially only focused on the visible challenges in her life, meaning the presenting issues; she did not realize the deeper root causes. By addressing the underlying entry points, she was able to begin a journey of healing and restoration. Through prayer, forgiveness, and the renewing of her mind, Laura found freedom from the stronghold that she had struggled with for so long.

When deliverance ministry focuses solely on dismantling the stronghold without addressing the legal right, it is like tearing down a house while the demon rebuilds it simultaneously. This creates a cycle of sin and confession: the person may do well for a few weeks or months, but they eventually fall back into the same pattern. They repent and confess, experience temporary relief, and then the cycle repeats. Without dealing with the legal right, the cycle remains unbroken. A legal right of entry always involves behavior: it is something the person did, said, or experienced (such as trauma or harm caused by others). In contrast, a stronghold consists of patterns of thinking and emotional responses within the person's soul. While a stronghold often influences behavior, its true power lies in how it shapes the person's emotions and thoughts.

This is why some individuals may intellectually understand that God loves them but cannot feel or experience His love. They might say, "I know He loves me," but they feel disconnected from that truth. Some may suggest to simply ignore our feelings and rely solely on faith, but God created us as emotional beings. Our emotions must be renewed and brought into alignment with the truth of God's Word. Dismantling a stronghold involves this renewal process which can only take place after addressing the legal right.

Once you identify the legal right, dealing with it is straightforward through confession and renunciation. By appropriating confession and renunciation in faith, the legal right is removed. However, discovering the legal right can be challenging as the enemy often buries or hides it behind a dominant stronghold or misleading thought patterns.

Removing a legal right through confession and renunciation is different from dismantling a stronghold. While the legal right can be addressed relatively quickly, strongholds require time, effort, and intentionality. Dismantling a stronghold involves renewing the mind through the Word of God, fellowship, and interaction with the Holy Spirit. A demon can be cast out of a person, but the stronghold may still remain. This is like evicting a demon from a house it built only to leave the structure intact. Renewing the mind and healing the emotions through inner healing is akin to renovating and restoring the house, thus ensuring that it is no longer a hospitable environment for the demon's return.

KINDS OF DEMONS

To effectively and thoroughly minister deliverance, it is important to understand the three primary categories of demonic spirits. Please note that I am not referencing principalities, powers, or global entities here, but rather demons that go by various names and carry specific characteristics. For example, if I reference a demon called Lucifer, I am not speaking about *the* Lucifer but a demon that identifies with the rank or name of Lucifer. This distinction is important because such demons have attained a certain level of wickedness that aligns with this title or rank.

It is not *the* Lucifer but *a* lucifer. The best way I can explain this is that demons carrying the title or rank of Lucifer operate with a higher level of wickedness and authority than, for instance, a spirit of infirmity. In this chapter, I will outline three broad categories into which demons can generally be classified. Understanding these categories will help you discern their functions, levels of authority, and degrees of wickedness.

TRAUMA-LEVEL DEMONS

The first type of demons we often encounter are what I call "trauma-level demons." As the name suggests, these demons operate to perpetuate trauma in a person's life and often enter through specific traumatic events. For example, I once ministered to someone who had been in a very traumatizing car accident. During the accident, he was overwhelmed by a gripping fear of death. As we walked him through deliverance, it became clear that a spirit of fear had entered during the pain and confusion surrounding the incident. The legal right of entry for the demon was rooted in fear rather than faith. Additionally, confusion, which is an emotional state that is not from God, further created another point of access in him. Demons often exploit such situations of vulnerability to gain entry.

Trauma-level demons frequently manifest as emotional and psychological burdens that work to deepen wounds caused by traumatic events. Some examples of demons in this category include spirits of shame, rejection, grief, heaviness, self-hatred, abuse, abandonment, loneliness, confusion, condemnation, sorrow, torment, doubt, isolation, and insecurity. These demons thrive on keeping individuals bound in patterns of despair, brokenness, and fear.

SIN-LEVEL DEMONS

The second category of demons is more apparent because they are tied directly to acts of sin and their functions. Common examples include spirits of lust, lying, hate, murder, fear, incest, abuse, molestation, perversion, anger, destruction, pride, suicide, death, rebellion, and violence. This list could go on and on as these demons thrive on keeping individuals ensnared in sinful behaviors and patterns.

When considering the authority these demons carry within the demonic hierarchy, sin-level and trauma-level demons are generally not among the highest-ranking entities. While they can wield significant power by feeding on strongholds and active sin in a person's life, they typically lack extensive kingdom structures or hierarchical authority over other demons. These "front-line demons" primarily function to keep a person trapped in sin and torment while protecting the higher-ranking, occult-level demons that we will discuss next.

Often, sin-level and trauma-level demons are the ones cast out during altar calls or moments of spontaneous deliverance in services. In such cases, the individual may have already repented and removed the legal rights that these demons had to remain. Once their legal rights are broken, a simple command in the name of Jesus, with perseverance, is often sufficient to cast them out. It is important to note that these types of demons are not typically the ones maintaining long-term, generational curses or holding entire bloodlines in bondage. Instead, they are usually tied to observable strongholds in an individual's life. These demons are what some refer to as the "low-hanging fruit" of deliverance as they are more easily identified and addressed.

However, this does not minimize the profound transformation that occurs when a person is freed from sin-level or trauma-level demons. Deliverance from these entities is still life-changing and brings freedom and healing to those who have been bound. Yet, it is also vital to recognize that there are higher-level demons, such as occult-level demons, which require a more strategic and thorough approach. These will be discussed in the next section.

OCCULT-LEVEL DEMONS

Occult-level demons are high-ranking entities often referred to by a proper or formal name. These are the chiefs, the bosses, and the top-tier, hierarchical demons that establish kingdoms within individuals. They are typically the ones that other demons serve, obey, and protect. These spirits are often anchored in long-term, multi-generational curses and are frequently tied to ancient civilizations. Their entry points are commonly associated with human sacrifices, animal sacrifices, blood covenants, or high-level occult curses placed upon individuals or families.

It is important to clarify that while these demons may share names with principalities that rule over territories, they are not necessarily the same. Just because a demon manifests with a name like "Lilith" during a deliverance session, it does not mean it is the ruling principality of the territory. In my experience, having conducted thousands of exorcisms, only on rare occasions have I been convinced that a territorial principality manifested through an individual. Do I believe it is possible for a principality to manifest through a person? Yes, I do. However, I do not believe it happens frequently. However, what can occur is that the repeated manifestation of demons with the same name, such as Lilith, within a specific territory may serve as spiritual intelligence: a revelation of the ruling principality of that area. Even so, this should not be taken as absolute proof. Such insights must be confirmed by the Holy Spirit and corroborated with other evidence.

The key point to understand is that while highly ranked, these occult-level demons are not necessarily principalities. They are spirits that we encounter that manifest daily through our deliverance ministry teams. There are countless names for these types of demons, but I will share a few to provide context for what is commonly encountered in deliverance sessions. Some of these names include Lucifer, Mammon, Baphomet, Apollyon, Abaddon, Antichrist, Asmodeus, Satan, Baal, Leviathan, Beelzebub, Python, Osiris, Isis, Ra, Horus, Set, Anubis, Zeus, Apollo, Diana, Artemis, Venus, Poseidon, Neptune, Ares, Hermes, Hades, Hecate, and the Queen of Heaven. The Queen of Heaven is known by many expressions including Aphrodite, Juno, Lilith, Asherah, Ishtar, and others. The list could continue endlessly, as there are thousands of such names. For more information on these demonic entities, see Chapter 5. These names and the characteristics associated with them provide insights into the nature and function of occult-level demons in deliverance ministry.

DEMONIC KINGDOMS

When we first began moving into a higher level of deliverance and realized the importance of thoroughly identifying the highest-ranking demon within a person, we noticed several distinct patterns emerging. One of the primary patterns was that demons not only operated according to their kind but were often structured within kingdoms. Let me clarify what I mean by "kind." This refers to categories like sin-level demons or trauma-level demons, as previously discussed. For example, if we encountered anger, it often ran alongside hatred, rage, and murder. These demons grouped and functioned together according to kind. Similarly, if we encountered perversion, we would often see homosexuality, rape, or other sin-based demons within the same category.

As we further delved into deliverance ministry, we began to recognize even stronger patterns of demons operating within organized kingdoms. While demons of the same kind often work together, a kingdom represents a larger, hierarchical structure where many different kinds of demons are arranged and operate under a specific order. To provide an example, I will list some basic demons often found within various kingdoms. This is by no means an exhaustive list as the number of demons within these kingdoms could easily reach into the thousands. However, understanding the key figures within these kingdoms allows us to discern their structures more effectively.

This recognition also applies across cultures and territories. Once you identify the top-ranking demons within a kingdom, you can quickly discern the hierarchical structure of that kingdom in any given region. As previously mentioned, many demonic kingdoms follow a hierarchical structure that mirrors a false trinity. Typically, we encounter a sun god, a moon goddess, and an enforcer spirit that is often serpent-like in nature. These three form a demonic "trinity" that governs the kingdom's operations.

ROMAN/GREEK DEMONIC KINGDOMS

Let me provide an example of how kingdoms might operate together. Consider a Roman or Greek kingdom. At the top of such a kingdom, one might find a high-ranking demon identified as Zeus or Jupiter. Beneath that, there could be other significant demons like Apollo, Diana (or Artemis), Aphrodite, Poseidon, or Kronos. These are all tied to prominent Roman and Greek gods and represent a structured hierarchy within the demonic realm. In this setup, the Roman or Greek kingdom may have Zeus at its head, with other demons organized beneath him, carrying out plans of destruction and oppression over the individual or their bloodline.

These higher-ranking occult-level demons establish the overarching structure of the kingdom. Beneath these top-tier demons, you will likely still encounter frontline demons such as those associated with murder, anger, lust, or perversion. However, these lower-level demons function in service to the higher-ranking ones, supporting the kingdom's schemes and maintaining its influence over the person's life.

CARIBBEAN/AFRICAN DEMONIC KINGDOM

In parts of the Caribbean and in Central and South America, particularly in regions historically impacted by slavery, it is common to find deep, spiritual roots anchored in African heritage. Within the African pantheon of demons, certain entities are frequently encountered in deliverance ministry. Among these, the spirit known as "Mami Wata" and the python serpent-spirit are often at the top of the hierarchy. Mami Wata is revered in various African spiritual traditions and is often associated with water, seduction, and wealth. She is a high-ranking spirit whose influence can extend into the generational bloodlines of those whose ancestors engaged in rituals or worship connected to her. On the other hand, the python spirit is a serpent-like entity often tied to deception, control, and oppression that symbolizes a powerful and insidious presence within the demonic hierarchy.

While these are prominent figures, there are many other demons within this spiritual framework that often go by different names depending on the region or cultural adaptation. Yet, a common thread persists: a serpent-spirit frequently rules within the bloodline. These bloodline curses are often anchored in human sacrifices and blood covenants. During times of enslavement, rituals and covenants were sometimes made by captors, enslaved individuals, or their descendants. These acts introduce deep, spiritual ties that can persist for generations. These covenants may have been forged in desperation, survival, or cultural practices, but the spiritual consequences remain active unless broken through the authority of Jesus Christ.

Understanding these roots is essential for effective deliverance. It allows ministers to address not only the surface-level manifestations but also the deeper, generational strongholds tied to these powerful entities. Deliverance must include breaking bloodline curses, renouncing covenants, and dismantling the authority of ruling spirits like Mami Wata and python to bring true freedom.

CENTRAL/SOUTH AMERICAN DEMONIC KINGDOMS

In Central and South America, demonic structures often vary significantly among the indigenous tribal peoples, yet many trace their roots back to Aztec or Mayan cultures. These civilizations were steeped in deep witchcraft practices and, in the case of the

Aztecs, human sacrifice was central to their devotion to their gods. The Aztecs were among the most dominant and bloodiest civilizations in history; human sacrifice was at the very heart of their religious practices.

One of the most infamous examples of this was the dedication of the Templo Mayor in 1487, under the rule of Aztec emperor, Ahuitzotl. This event, held in Tenochtitlán (modern-day Mexico City), is one of history's most striking examples of demonic devotion.[145] The Templo Mayor was dedicated to two primary gods of the Aztec pantheon: Huitzilopochtli, the god of war and the sun, and Tlaloc, the god of rain and fertility.[146] These gods demanded sacrificial offerings as a means of sustaining their power and ensuring the continuation of the cosmos, according to Aztec beliefs.

When ministering to individuals with ancestral ties to Mexico or Central and South America, we often encounter curses that trace back to such rituals, particularly those tied to Aztec practices. While it is rare to see Huitzilopochtli manifest during deliverance sessions, other prominent spirits frequently surface. Quetzalcoatl, the Feathered Serpent, is a common manifestation, along with Chicomacoatl and Tlaloc. These spirits are deeply rooted in ancestral bloodlines, often tied to the sacrifices and covenants made during those ancient practices.

NORDIC DEMONIC KINGDOMS

We live in East Tennessee, and many of the family bloodlines that immigrated and settled in our region trace their ancestry back to the Nordic nations. One of the most dominant patterns we see in deliverance sessions with individuals from these bloodlines is the manifestations of demons tied to Norse mythology. Common spirits include Odin, Thor, Loki, Freya, Fenrir, and others associated with the ancient Nordic pantheon.

OTHER DEMONIC KINGDOMS

There is no need for me to list every possible kingdom or demonic structure that you may encounter. This is an area where you can conduct your own research, particularly if you find yourself ministering in geographical regions or working with individuals whose bloodlines trace back to specific cultures or areas. Do not hesitate to do a simple search for the traditional gods worshiped in those regions. It is amazing at how uncovering this information can reveal ancient bloodline curses tied to these demonic entities during deliverance sessions.

If this is your first time encountering this level of detail, I understand that it might feel overwhelming or hard to grasp. You might be tempted to default back to simply casting demons out without digging deeper. While this approach can sometimes work, truly thorough and effective deliverance ministry often requires a systematic approach, guided by the Holy Spirit, to dismantle these demonic structures completely. Let me re-emphasize an earlier point: while deliverance is critical for the individual in front of you, its significance often extends far beyond just that person.

Deliverance can bring freedom, not only to entire families and bloodlines, but also to regions and territories. When these structures are dismantled within a person, the spiritual intelligence revealed may be a key to breaking strongholds over an entire family or even an entire region. Please do not dismiss this information as trivial or overly complex. It is a vital part of understanding how to operate effectively in deliverance ministry and address the deeper, more systemic roots of bondage.

CHAPTER 7

SPIRITUAL WARFARE AND CORRELATION BETWEEN CURSES AND DELIVERANCE

I cannot emphasize enough the correlation between effective, thorough deliverance ministry and the breaking of curses. I would estimate that as many as 85 percent of the cases we deal with in casting out demons are directly tied to curses within the bloodline. Recently, I was contacted by a Native American minister who had already undergone extensive deliverance but was still struggling, particularly with torment during sleep. This individual had a successful ministry, was not living in sin, and appeared healthy and stable by all outward measures. However, she was plagued by recurring bloody and gory dreams in which demons would appear and speak tormenting curses over her.

As I began ministering to this person, I led her in renouncing bloodline curses tied to ancestral blood sacrifices offered to demons. Almost immediately, a demon manifested and revealed that it had entered six generations earlier when one of her grandfathers, who was a tribal shaman, summoned an ancestral god and sealed a blood covenant with it. The shaman had performed an animal blood sacrifice and dedicated the next eight generations to the demon in exchange for power to defeat their enemies in battle. Once this blood covenant was uncovered through a brief demonic interrogation, I guided the individual to renounce the agreement and break the curse over herself and her bloodline. As soon as the renunciation was complete, the demon declared it had no further legal rights to the person. We were then able to cast out the demon and its entire kingdom!

This testimony highlights the critical importance of understanding bloodline curses in deliverance ministry. Despite having ministered deliverance to many others, this person struggled with her own freedom due to a lack of understanding about curses. The process of breaking the curse and expelling the demon took less than 45 minutes, yet she had endured great torment since childhood. While a previous deliverance had addressed some lower-level demons, no one had identified and dealt with the chief demon of the kingdom or the curse that gave it the right and power to torment her.

In one instance, a minister came to me for a deliverance session. The night before her arrival, I had a dream where I saw a curse connected to the Spaniard conquest of an Asian nation. Although the specifics of the curse were unclear, I knew it involved the Spanish and that her bloodline traced back to this Asian nation. I kept this in mind as we proceeded with the session. The session started smoothly. We closed doors, broke general curses, and eventually, the demon Lucifer—*a* lucifer, not *the* Lucifer—manifested. This particular demon declared it had a legal right going back about four generations that was tied to a blood sacrifice of an animal. We broke that curse, but I kept the Spanish connection in mind.

As I pressed further, I commanded the demon, "Do you have any further legal rights or curses in this bloodline? Yes or no?" Eventually, the demon cried out, "Yes, I have a right!" When I demanded it to specify the legal right, the demon revealed that it was tied to the Spanish control of the nation. It related specifically to a forced marriage in her bloodline which was a way for the demon to gain entry into this Asian nation's lineage. After binding the demon, we broke this older curse, which spanned approximately seven generations. With the legal right removed, we cast out the demon and its kingdom. The person has walked in freedom ever since.

SPIRITUAL WARFARE AND CURSES

Much of Western society has lost a supernatural worldview and thus, relegated spiritual warfare to mundane inconveniences. I often joke that Western Christians might close their hand in a car door, smash their finger, and declare that Satan is against them that day. In truth, we have reduced spiritual warfare down to mere ignorance or human error. However, true spiritual warfare is far more profound; it is a literal confrontation between the powers of darkness and the Kingdom of Light. Spiritual warfare involves entities whose sole purpose is to steal, kill, and destroy. It is imperative that we elevate our understanding and maturity to grasp the true nature of this battle.

Recently, I experienced a season that underscored the reality of spiritual warfare in a powerful way. After an intense period of travel filled with equipping churches and speaking at conferences, I came home utterly exhausted. During what should have been a time of rest, I began to experience severe physical sickness, including a diverticulitis flare-up. By the fourth day, the pain became excruciating and was radiating throughout my body. It was so severe that I found myself lying on the couch, crying out to God in desperation: "I don't even have the words to pray, but this hurts so badly!"

This torment lasted for nine days. Around that time, our intercessors were on high alert, praying fervently for me. Then, a prophetic friend, who was completely unaware of my situation, sent me a message about a dream that he had the previous night. In the dream, he was taken to a witchcraft store in our neighboring town, a store we had been praying against for some time due to the demonic activity there. Above the store, he saw its sign, and inside, the practitioners had constructed an old water well. They were pouring potions into the well while chanting incantations and calling upon Lilith.

Lilith was a ruling principality in our territory and one that we have been contending with for years. As I read his message, it became clear that this ritual in the dream symbolized targeted curses being sent against me. These were aimed at destroying me as the senior leader of The Well. What I was experiencing was not just natural sickness; it was a coordinated spiritual attack. This was spiritual warfare on a deeper level as we began warring against curses that they had spoken over my life. It took several more days of focused prayer and intercession to fully break the attack.

The purpose of sharing this experience is to elevate your understanding and maturity concerning spiritual warfare. It is essential to prepare yourself as we delve into what curses are and how they operate. Recognizing the spiritual dynamics at work allows us to stand firm and equipped to combat the schemes of the enemy with the authority and power of Christ.

WHAT IS A CURSE?

Before defining a curse, it is important to understand that there are many types of curses that we encounter in deliverance ministry. These include divine judgment curses, general and specific curses, intentional and unintentional curses, land and water curses, and curses triggered by specific circumstances. Each operates differently, and understanding these distinctions is vital for ministering effectively.

A curse can be defined as the summoning or alignment with demonic forces to release an assignment against a person, family, or bloodline. A curse is essentially an agreement or contract within the demonic realm to bring about a specific result in the natural realm. However, there is a distinction between a curse and a demon. Demons carry out the agreement established by the curse, but they are not the curse itself. Think of a curse as a conduit for a demon's operation and as a means for demons to ride upon. A person may be under a curse without being internally demonized.

For example, I once ministered to a doctor who was also a minister. He experienced severe physical sensations that led to anxiety and panic, yet medical tests revealed no physical cause for his symptoms. During a deliverance session, we addressed curse-breaking and closed all legal doors through repentance and renunciation. No demonic manifestations occurred nor was there evidence of internal demonization. However, after breaking the curses, the doctor's symptoms disappeared immediately. This demonstrates that curses alone, without internal demons, can cause significant distress. When broken, the effects of these curses vanish thus reducing spiritual warfare in the person's life.

Curses can vary greatly in strength depending on how they were enacted. For example, a curse enacted through witchcraft and aimed at causing specific harm may not result in internal demonization but can still manifest in a person's life as spiritual warfare. Curses can also be unintentional and arise from agreements made in ignorance. While such curses may initially be weak, they can grow stronger as the person's thoughts and actions deepen their agreement with the curse's intent. As believers in Christ, we do not need to fear curses. We walk in the authority and power of Jesus knowing that the blood of Christ cleanses us of sin and closes all doors to the enemy. Proverbs 26:2 reminds us, "*Like a sparrow in its flitting, like a swallow in its flying, so a curse without cause does not come to rest.*"

When Andrea and I moved to Haiti as missionaries in 2009, we encountered an intense level of darkness unlike anything we had faced before. Five voodoo temples surrounded our home, and the spiritual climate was thick with demonic activity. Night after night, we heard the rhythms of voodoo drums as people worshiped serpent spirits and actively sought demon possession. This provoked us in the spirit to intercede and evangelize in the area by proclaiming the Gospel. As we persisted, voodoo temples began to shut down, but the spiritual warfare intensified.

One night, as we slept on our roof to avoid the dangers of concrete buildings following the earthquake of 2010, we heard voodoo drums growing louder and saw torches approaching our home. A group surrounded our property, chanting, dancing, and drinking blood in an attempt to curse and intimidate us. Yet, we stood firm on the promise of Proverbs 26:2 as we knew that their curses could not land without a cause. Through prayer and faith, we resisted their attempts, and their curses had no effect.

The next morning, at 6:00 AM, I knocked on the voodoo priest's door. When he answered groggily, I introduced myself as the missionary he had tried to curse. I proclaimed the power of the resurrected Christ within me and informed him that his practices would no longer be tolerated in the territory. I told him that he had two choices: repent and come to faith in Jesus or leave the area. Shortly after this confrontation, he left the region entirely.

This experience highlights the authority we have in Christ and the power of curse-breaking. Fear empowers demons, but faith puts them in their place. When we operate in the authority of Christ and the truth of His Word, we overcome the enemy, break curses, and walk in freedom.

TYPES OF CURSES

DIVINE JUDGMENT CURSES

When many Christians hear the word *curse,* oftentimes, they immediately think of divine judgment curses. It is true that Jesus Himself broke the curse of the Law and sin and empowers us to deal with other types of curses. However, without a deeper understanding of the various kinds of curses, some may dismiss the idea altogether and believe that Jesus has already resolved every curse completely. This belief stems from the truth that Jesus has redeemed us from the curse of sin. The curse of sin, rooted in humanity's rebellion against God, represents a divine judgment curse pronounced by God as a consequence of disobedience in the Garden of Eden. We read about the warning of this in Genesis 2:15-17:

> *Then the Lord God took the man and put him in the Garden of Eden to cultivate it and tend it. The Lord God commanded*

the man, saying, "From any tree of the garden you may freely eat; but from the tree of the knowledge of good and evil you shall not eat, for on the day that you eat from it you will certainly die."

And we all know the story of how Adam and Eve disobeyed God and God released a curse in Genesis 3:14–19 (NLT):

Then the Lord God said to the serpent, "Because you have done this, you are cursed more than all animals, domestic and wild. You will crawl on your belly, groveling in the dust as long as you live. And I will cause hostility between you and the woman, and between your offspring and her offspring. He will strike your head, and you will strike his heel." Then he said to the woman, "I will sharpen the pain of your pregnancy, and in pain you will give birth. And you will desire to control your husband, but he will rule over you." And to the man he said, "Since you listened to your wife and ate from the tree whose fruit I commanded you not to eat, the ground is cursed because of you. All your life you will struggle to scratch a living from it. It will grow thorns and thistles for you, though you will eat of its grains. By the sweat of your brow will you have food to eat until you return to the ground from which you were made. For you were made from dust, and to dust you will return."

In these passages, God Himself placed a clear warning upon humanity: if they ate from the tree, they would die. The disobedience of Adam and Eve unleashed a divine judgment curse of death upon mankind. But God did not stop there. He spoke directly to the woman and warned her of pain in childbirth and against her desire to control her husband; to Adam, He revealed that the ground itself was now cursed because of his disobedience. Finally, God declared, "You are dust, and to dust you will return," which explicitly refers to physical death.

This original sin and disobedience to God resulted in a divine judgment curse that has affected all of humanity and the very land of the earth. It is important to recognize that the origin of this curse is God Himself. While man's disobedience was the catalyst, it was God who pronounced this judgment thus bringing death upon humanity and cursing the ground because of sin.

Now, let's explore a parallel situation regarding blessings for obedience and curses for disobedience, specifically in the Mosaic Covenant (also known as the Law of Moses or the Old Covenant). To summarize, the Law of Moses functioned as a covenant in which obedience brought blessings and disobedience brought curses. Much like the situation in the Garden of Eden, obedience to God's commands resulted in life and blessings while disobedience led to curses. This principle is laid out in Deuteronomy 28:1-2 (NIV):

> *If you fully obey the Lord your God and carefully follow all his commands I give you today, the Lord your God will set you high above all the nations on earth. All these blessings will come on you and accompany you if you obey the Lord your God.*

In contrast, verse 15 (NIV) warns:

> *However, if you do not obey the Lord your God and do not carefully follow all his commands and decrees I am giving you today, all these curses will come on you and overtake you.*

It is crucial to note the source of these curses in divine judgment curses. While human disobedience triggers them, these curses are pronounced directly by God. I must emphasize that when we engage in breaking curses, we are not addressing divine judgment curses from God. The curse of death resulting from original sin and the curses for disobedience under the Law of Moses are the very curses that Jesus dealt with on the cross. Through His death and resurrection, Jesus redeemed us from the curse of sin and the curse of the Law thus fulfilling what humanity could not achieve on its own.

JESUS BROKE THE CURSE OF SIN AND OF THE LAW OF MOSES

As I referenced before, when Christians hear the word *curse or curses,* they often assume that Jesus has dealt with all curses entirely. In reality, what they are referring to is the curse of sin and the curse of the Law. On this point, I am in 100 percent agreement that Jesus has dealt with both the curse of sin and the curse associated with the Law. This is forever settled in heaven, as we have been brought into a better covenant that is founded upon better promises.

The following several scriptures are all taken from the New International Version. Galatians 3:10 reminds us: *"For all who rely on the works of the law are under a curse, as it is written: 'Cursed is everyone who does not continue to do everything written in the Book of the Law.'"* Verses 13-14 further explain:

> *Christ redeemed us from the curse of the Law by becoming a curse for us, for it is written: "Cursed is everyone who is hung on a pole." He redeemed us in order that the blessing given to Abraham might come to the Gentiles through*

Christ Jesus, so that by faith we might receive the promise of the Spirit.

Romans 8:1-2 further affirms this truth: *"Therefore, there is now no condemnation for those who are in Christ Jesus, because through Christ Jesus the law of the Spirit who gives life has set you free from the law of sin and death."* The apostle Paul reflects on the Law in Romans 7:10-11: *"I found that the very commandment that was intended to bring life actually brought death. For sin, seizing the opportunity afforded by the commandment, deceived me, and through the commandment put me to death."* In 2 Corinthians 3:6, Paul contrasts the old and new covenants: *"He has made us competent as ministers of a new covenant—not of the letter but of the Spirit; for the letter kills, but the Spirit gives life."* In Romans 4:15, Paul highlights the limitations of the Law: *"because the law brings wrath. And where there is no law there is no transgression."*

Colossians 2:13-14 gloriously declares: *"When you were dead in your sins and in the uncircumcision of your flesh, God made you alive with Christ. He forgave us all our sins, having canceled the charge of our legal indebtedness, which stood against us and condemned us; he has taken it away, nailing it to the cross."* Hebrews 7:18-19 contrasts the law with the hope we now have through Christ: *"The former regulation is set aside because it was weak and useless (for the law made nothing perfect), and a better hope is introduced, by which we draw near to God."* Finally, Romans 6:14 assures us: *"For sin shall no longer be your master, because you are not under the law, but under grace."*

This collection of scriptures emphasizes that the curse of the Law and the curse of sin have been decisively dealt with by Jesus. Through His death and resurrection, we have been set free from the Law of sin and death. Now, we live under grace in the New Covenant that offers life and hope.

SPIRITUAL WARFARE AND TERRITORIAL CURSES

In deliverance ministry, we often encounter two primary types of spiritual warfare: ground-level spiritual warfare and strategic-level spiritual warfare. Ground-level warfare focuses primarily on delivering individuals from demons. This work often extends to the families or bloodlines and also addresses generational strongholds. When handled thoroughly and with discernment, the spiritual intelligence gained from these encounters often leads to strategic-level spiritual warfare. Strategic-level spiritual warfare moves beyond the individual and targets broader regions, territories, or systemic strongholds. This involves discerning why certain lands or regions remain cursed and identifying the strongholds that perpetuate these curses. Often, these territorial strongholds result from collective agreements made by the people of a region with ruling spiritual entities.

I believe we are entering a time of spiritual maturity when ground-level warfare and strategic-level warfare will no longer operate independently. God is raising up teams equipped to integrate both of these ministries and simultaneously deliver individuals and families while also dismantling territorial strongholds. This unity will advance the Kingdom of God and bring forth great freedom to both people and regions. As we move forward in deliverance ministry, it is critical to discern where spiritual warfare originates. Assuming that one has broken curses and been delivered from internal demonization, spiritual warfare will primarily come from two sources that we will discuss next.

SPIRITUAL WARFARE FROM ADVANCING THE GOSPEL (GROUND-LEVEL WARFARE)

Engaging in ground-level deliverance ministry often provokes spiritual warfare as you advance the Gospel in the lives of individuals, families, and bloodlines. This type of warfare frequently manifests through dreams, night encounters, or visions intended to intimidate or instill fear. When direct attacks fail, the enemy often shifts to distorting relationships and introducing confusion or division between you and those God has called you to partner with. This is why maintaining strong, honorable relationships within your team and your family is essential. A united front prevents these tactics from piercing the relational veil.

SPIRITUAL WARFARE FROM TERRITORIAL SPIRITS (STRATEGIC-LEVEL WARFARE)

Territorial spirits ruling over regions often target individuals that enter their domain. This type of warfare can manifest simply because your presence in a cursed or spiritually defiled territory disrupts the established control. Such opposition does not necessarily mean that you are directly engaging the territorial spirit but does reveal the broader, strategic-level conflict tied to the region. I refer to this as a triggered curse. These curses are not personal but activate when a man or woman of God steps into a territory controlled by a principality. For instance, in Acts 16:16, Paul encountered a slave girl possessed by a spirit of Python. The spirit began following him, creating annoyance and distraction for several days. This encounter illustrates how Paul's presence in Philippi, which was a spiritually defiled region, triggered demonic resistance.

Importantly to note, Paul did not immediately confront the spirit. Instead, he waited for the Lord's timing to enter this higher level of warfare. In Acts 16:16 (NIV) describes this encounter: "*Once when we were going to the place of prayer, we were met by a female slave who had a spirit by which she predicted the future. She earned a great deal of money for her owners by fortune-telling.*" This event demonstrates the resistance encountered in regions dominated by territorial spirits and further underscores the need for discernment and timing in spiritual warfare.

Rebecca Greenwood, in her book *Authority to Tread*, offers profound insights into territorial warfare. She describes how confronting territorial spirits requires not only authority in Christ but also strategic wisdom. Her work highlights the importance of understanding the spiritual climate of a region and the strongholds that maintain its oppression. Greenwood writes:

> Paul and Silas in Philippi: According to Greek legend, the Greek god Apollo killed Python, the terrible earth serpent who lived in the caves of Parnassus in Delphi. He killed Python in retaliation for its harassment of his mother while she was looking for a place to give birth to her twins. Because of his act Apollo is at times referred to as Pythian, predictor of future events.
>
> During Paul's day the people in the region of Philippi believed that Apollo or Pythian was the influencer of events. The term python was used to refer to those through whom the python spirit spoke. We read in the book of Acts that Paul entered into spiritual warfare by casting out this python or fortune-telling spirit from a slave girl (see Acts 16:18). This caused great turmoil in the city of Philippi. It is my belief

that the response and activities that occurred as a result of Paul's prayer indicate that the spirit operating through this young woman was indeed a territorial spirit. Let me explain what I mean. Acts 16:19 says that when the owners of the slave girl realized what had occurred they became greatly disturbed. It ruined their opportunity to make money from those seeking information about the future.

They seized Paul and Silas and brought them before the authorities in the marketplace. In verse 20 (NIV) the slave owners stated, *"These men are Jews, and are **throwing our city into an uproar**"* (emphasis added). I find this accusation highly interesting. Paul addressed a demonic spirit operating through a young girl. Next he was accused of throwing a whole city into an uproar.

I have prayed deliverance prayers over many individuals, but never has it resulted in a city uproar. Then we read in verse 22: "The crowd joined in the attack against Paul and Silas." Not only was the whole city in an uproar, but now a crowd joined in the attack against Paul and Silas. Why would casting out a demon from one girl cause a city uproar and a crowd, who knew nothing of the deliverance, to turn against Paul and Silas? The python spirit operating through this slave girl or spiritist was a territorial spirit that gripped the city of Philippi.

The magistrates ordered that Paul and Silas be flogged and thrown into prison. Locked in an inner cell with their feet fastened in stocks, Paul and Silas began to pray and worship God.

Let's investigate what occurred next. "Suddenly there was such a *violent earthquake* that the foundations of the prison were shaken. At once all the prison doors flew open, and everybody's chains came loose" (Acts 16:26, emphasis added).

Wow! As a result of casting out this demonic spirit in a slave girl, a violent earthquake occurred over the region. Not only were Paul's and Silas's chains released, but everybody's chains came loose. When effective spiritual warfare prayer has occurred, signs of what has transpired in the spiritual realm will also manifest in the physical realm—thus, the earthquake.

God was shaking the foundational worship of Apollo in that region. The earthquake resulted in everybody's chains releasing. Another indication of effective spiritual warfare prayer is the release of the people of the region from the darkness that has gripped them. They are then free to understand and experience the truth and love of God.

Note the breakthrough that occurred in this spiritual warfare encounter in Philippi:

The jailer called for lights, rushed in and fell trembling before Paul and Silas. He then brought them out and asked, "Sirs, what must I do to be saved?" They replied, "Believe in the Lord Jesus, and you will be saved—you and your household." Then they spoke the word of the Lord to him and to all the others in his house. At that hour of the night the jailer took them and washed their wounds; then immediately he and all his family were baptized. The jailer brought them into his house and set a meal before them; he was filled with joy because he had come to believe in God—he and his whole family (verses 29-34).

The most significant demonstration that spiritual breakthrough has occurred over a region is the salvation of those who have been trapped in spiritual darkness by a territorial spirit.

Let's review this spiritual warfare encounter. Paul cast out a python spirit, also called a spirit of divination, from a slave girl. The resulting actions were a city uproar, an angry crowd, the imprisonment of Paul and Silas, a violent earthquake that released everybody's chains and the salvation of the jailer and his family. It is obvious that the spirit in this young woman was indeed a territorial spirit that held this region in darkness.[147]

Territorial spirits cannot simply assume authority except in the absent or neglected authority of Christians over an area. Just as a demon cannot enter an individual without a cause or a legal right of entry, the same principle applies to territorial spirits. There must be some form of agreement between the people dwelling on the land and the territorial power that grants the spirit the legal right to rule. Once the territorial spirit gains this authority, it draws the people into deeper bondage and results in spiritual oppression and the "locking up" of the land. There are four primary factors that commonly grant rulership to a territorial spirit.

1. SHEDDING OF INNOCENT BLOOD

The shedding of innocent blood is one of the most severe sins that defiles the land and causes it to cry out to God for justice. This includes murder, abortion, occult practices involving human sacrifice, and even the cruelty and injustice of certain wars. Genesis 4:10 (NIV) illustrates this principle when God confronts Cain: "*The Lord said, 'What have you done? Listen! Your brother's blood cries out to me from the ground.'*" Blood unjustly spilled creates a spiritual stain upon the land. Practices like systemic violence or legalized abortion perpetuate this defilement and require repentance and intercession to bring cleansing and healing.

Our ministry recently began working in the nation of Cambodia. Before formally launching this work, some friends and I took a private, low-key trip to the country to test what God had placed on our hearts. The morning after our arrival, I woke up early to pray over the capital city of Phnom Penh. As I interceded, God gave me a vision of two large warring monkeys which reminded me of Hanuman, the god of war from Indian mythology. These monkeys had grimacing expressions of anger, and their eyes were fixed directly on me. They raised their hands high in the air and stomped the ground, rocking back and forth as though trying to intimidate me.

In that moment, I felt the weight of their intimidation, but even more, I felt the righteous anger of the Lord rising up within me. As I continued to pray, I began to hear the blood crying out from the land. It was one of the most profound spiritual experiences of my life. The blood cried out for the Lord of Justice to come, and its anguishing cry penetrated my being. I was overwhelmed by the deep injustice that had been committed against the people and the land. Through that moment of intercession, God birthed within me His heart for the nation of Cambodia.

Cambodia's history is absolutely tragic, and it is a land that has endured immense suffering. Under the Khmer Rouge regime, nearly 50 percent of the population was murdered in a horrific genocide from 1975 to 1979. Today, Cambodia remains one of the youngest nations on the planet by average age. These young generations are locked within the systems of Buddhism and Hinduism. Yet, I know that the Lord of Justice is coming to bring freedom and awakening to that land. His plans are for restoration, and I believe we are on the cusp of seeing His righteousness and mercy transform Cambodia.

2. BROKEN COVENANTS

Broken covenants, whether between nations, people groups, or within marriages, defile the land and create long-lasting spiritual repercussions. Violations like broken treaties between indigenous peoples and settlers often leave spiritual wounds that persist across generations. Marriage, as a covenant ordained by God, holds special significance. Malachi 2:14-15 underscores this:

> *Yet you say, "For what reason?" Because the Lord has been a witness between you and the wife of your youth, against whom you have dealt treacherously, though she is your marriage companion and your wife by covenant. But not one has done so who has a remnant of the Spirit. And why the one? He was seeking a godly offspring. Be careful then about your spirit, and see that none of you deals treacherously against the wife of your youth.*

Violating marriage covenants introduces spiritual rifts that affect families and communities. Restoring the sanctity of these covenants through repentance is key to breaking the curses that result.

3. SEXUAL IMMORALITY

Sexual immorality defiles the land profoundly as it violates God's design for purity and relationships. Prostitution, adultery, perversion, incest, rape, and molestation are among the sins that create spiritual contamination. Leviticus 18:25 attests of this: "*For the land has become defiled, therefore I have brought its punishment upon it, so the land has vomited out its inhabitants.*" The sins of Sodom and Gomorrah exemplify how unchecked immorality invites divine judgment. This collective guilt highlights the need for repentance, both personally and corporately, to cleanse the land and break the grip of these spiritual strongholds.

4. IDOLATRY AND WITCHCRAFT

Idolatry, witchcraft, cults, and false religions empower demonic forces and further defile the land. When communities worship false gods or engage in occult practices, they establish spiritual agreements that bind the land to darkness. Deuteronomy 12:2-3 gives clear instructions:

> *You shall utterly destroy all the places where the nations whom you are going to dispossess serve their gods, on the high mountains, on the hills, and under every leafy tree. And you shall tear down their altars and smash their memorial stones to pieces, and burn their Asherim in the fire, and cut to pieces the carved images of their gods; and you shall eliminate their name from that place.*

Such practices often involve rituals and sacrifices that entrench territorial spirits. Cleansing these defilements requires prayer, fasting, and strategic spiritual warfare to dismantle these agreements and reclaim the land and the people for God.

MOVING TOWARD RESTORATION

To heal defiled land, believers must engage in repentance, prayer, and spiritual warfare. Recognizing the specific sins tied to the land enables us to pray targeted prayers that dismantle these strongholds. God promises restoration in 2 Chronicles 7:14: "*And if My people who are called by My name humble themselves, and pray and seek My face, and turn from their wicked ways, then I will hear from heaven, and I will forgive their sin and will heal their land.*" Addressing these root causes of defilement brings healing, not only to the land, but also to the people who inhabit it.

Some curses are specific and intentional while others have more general origins. Additionally, there are curses that are triggered when certain circumstances arise. These triggers can be tied to factors such as time, age, or other conditions in a person's life. All these curses may be directed toward an individual, a family, a bloodline, or even specific groups of people.

UNINTENTIONAL CURSES

Unintentional curses often originate through the ignorance of people. These curses may arise from specific acts of violence, abuse, or hatred, but they can also begin during traumatic events in an individual or a family's life. Such curses can stem from the actions of either the perpetrator of a violent act or the recipient of that act. For example, I have encountered numerous cases where previous generations were involved in prostitution. This led to curses of sexual abuse and perversion being perpetuated in subsequent generations.

One particular event stands out concerning this. At the conclusion of a service where I was leading the congregation in curse-breaking declarations, a man named Fred came forward and was already manifesting a demon. When I approached him, I bound the demon and commanded it to go down and remain silent so I could speak with Fred directly. I asked Fred what was happening, and he responded, "All I can see is the Burning Man."

Curious and concerned, I asked him to explain further. Fred shared that in his family, there was a strange tradition: young children were often asked if they had seen the Burning Man, either in person or in their dreams. While no one in the family knew the origin of this phenomenon, it was common for children between the ages of five and eight to eventually report seeing the Burning Man. Over time, this occurrence almost became a celebration within the family.

As Fred relayed this story, I felt a deep concern in my spirit. I suggested that we renounce the Burning Man and break any associated curse. I led Fred in a prayer of renunciation and had him cut off all ties to the Burning Man. At that moment, the demon, Lucifer, manifested. During a brief and limited interrogation of the demon, it was revealed that several generations earlier, a house fire had occurred in Fred's family during which a person was burned alive. While this event had been forgotten over time, its traumatic spiritual impact had not. Following the fire, members of the family began to see the Burning Man, which was actually a manifestation of Lucifer. Instead of addressing this spiritual intrusion, out of their ignorance, the family allowed it to persist and in a bizarre manner, even celebrated the appearance of this demonic vision.

This situation illustrates a prime example of an unintentional curse. Because the family failed to confront the trauma and the spiritual consequences of the event, a curse was perpetuated in the bloodline, granting Lucifer a foothold. After leading Fred in renouncing the Burning Man and breaking the associated curse, we cast out Lucifer and his kingdom. Fred left the service completely free and was walking in the newfound freedom that only Christ can provide.

SPOKEN WORD CURSES

Often, we are required to break curses spoken over people typically done by those in authority in their lives. For example, parents who unintentionally align with demonic influence can speak words of death or destruction over their children thus creating curses. Parents hold a God-given authority over their children, like a spiritual "power of attorney," so to speak. When they misuse that authority by speaking negatively, even unintentionally, they can grant permission in the spiritual realm for demons to act through the curse and bring destruction upon the child's life. Proverbs 18:21 reminds us of the power of words: "*Death and life are in the power of the tongue, and those who love it will eat its fruit.*" Careless or harmful words spoken by those in authority carry significant spiritual weight.

One such instance involved a woman who came forward during an altar service. Shame and self-hatred were evident in her demeanor; she could barely look up as she approached me. I gently asked her, "Why do you hate yourself?" Though it was difficult for her to speak, she eventually opened up and explained that whenever she looked at herself in the mirror, she would hear the voices of her mother and father saying things like, "You're ugly," "No one will ever love you," and other destructive statements.

It took some time, but I first led her to forgive her parents for the hurtful words they had spoken over her following the example of Ephesians 4:31-32: "*All bitterness, wrath, anger, shouting, and slander must be removed from you, along with all malice. Be kind to one another, compassionate, forgiving each other, just as God in Christ also has forgiven you.*" Forgiveness was the first step to breaking the stronghold. Next, we renounced those curses and broke her agreement with the belief system her parents' words had created.

Proverbs 12:18 highlights this process: "*One who speaks rashly is like the thrusts of a sword, but the tongue of the wise brings healing.*"

Once the legal rights of the demons were removed, we cast them out of her in Jesus's name. By the end of that encounter, she was able to declare with confidence that she was a beautiful woman and was free from the pain and tormenting voices that had haunted her for so long. This story illustrates how unintended curses can be spoken through careless words, especially when uttered by those in positions of authority.

INTENTIONAL CURSES

Intentional curses are often far more powerful and direct than unintentional ones. These curses arise when a human being consciously partners with demonic spirits to release harm or destruction upon an individual, family, or group. Intentional curses can be highly specific, sometimes tied to particular times, events, or outcomes. Such curses are frequently associated with secret societies like Freemasonry, the Eastern Star, and the Mormon Church, as well as occult practices found in Wicca, Santeria, Voodoo, African pagan religions, Hinduism, and many others. For Christians in Western cultures, this concept might seem foreign or exaggerated due to desensitization to the spiritual realm. However, believers from regions like Africa or Asia are often acutely aware of the reality and power of these intentional curses.

During a recent ministry session with a prophetic minister, we encountered a striking example of an intentional curse. As we engaged in breaking curses, the man began to experience extreme pain in his hands, crying out, "Help me, my hands are on fire!" This was not a manifestation of God's refining fire but the oppressive torment of something deeply evil. As we pressed into the deliverance process, the demon, Baal, manifested.

Through a brief and limited interrogation, it was revealed that eight generations prior, a group of witches in a Nordic nation had placed a curse upon this man's bloodline. The curse was specifically aimed at silencing prophets in his lineage and preventing them from speaking the word of the Lord. After leading him to break the curse in the name of Jesus, we bound Baal along with its kingdom and cast them all out. Since that moment, the man has walked in complete freedom and was fully restored to his prophetic calling.

This testimony is not unique in our ministry. Stories of such specificity in curses and deliverance are not extraordinary for us; they are part of the spiritual battles we encounter daily. One particularly intense case involved a former Satanist and high-ranking witch who sought deliverance at our church. After extended deliverance ministry, we reached a standstill. In such cases, unresolved deliverance is often tied to a hidden shame or unconfessed sin that blocks the process.

After reassuring this individual of God's love and our desire to see her free, she confessed something shocking: she revealed that she had attempted to place a death curse upon me and offered an animal sacrifice to a demon as part of the ritual. To my astonishment, she brought forward the very dagger that was used in the sacrifice. Of course, the curse had no effect on me because of the protective power of Christ as previously discussed from Proverbs 26:2. I assured her that I harbored no anger or ill-will toward her and had already forgiven her for these actions. Once the confession was complete, we proceeded to cast out the demons and ultimately, led her to full freedom in Jesus's name.

These stories illustrate the reality of spiritual warfare. It is not merely a metaphor but a literal conflict between opposing spiritual forces. As Christians, we must recognize this reality and understand that through Jesus Christ, we have absolute authority over every demonic force. Jesus declared in Luke 10:19, "*Behold, I have given you authority to walk on snakes and scorpions, and authority over all the power of the enemy, and nothing will injure you.*" We are equipped to prevail in these battles, not by our own strength but through the unmatched power and authority found in the name of Jesus Christ. This authority and power enables us to confront curses, break their hold, and release those bound by demonic oppression into the freedom and victory of God's Kingdom.

INTENTIONAL BIBLICAL CURSE

There is a strong example in Scripture of how demonic power can be released through an intentional curse fueled by human sacrifice to a false god. In 2 Kings 3, the king of Israel joined forces with the kings of Edom and Judah to wage war against the Moabites. The god of the Moabites, Chemosh, closely resembled Baal and Moloch in the worship practices associated with him, including human sacrifice. As the three allied nations advanced against the Moabites, victory seemed assured. However, in a desperate and wicked act, the Moabite king took his eldest son, who was the heir to his throne, and sacrificed him as a burnt offering to Chemosh. This horrific act unleashed a powerful, spiritual shift, and scripture records that great wrath was released against Israel. Following the sacrifice, the tide of the battle turned, and the Moabites began to prevail. Second Kings 3:21-27 (AMP) describes this story:

Now all the Moabites heard that the [three] kings had come up to fight against them, and all who were able to put on armor, as well as those who were older, were summoned and stood [together in battle formation] at the border. When they got up early the next morning, the sun shone on the water, and the Moabites saw the water across from them as red as blood. And they said, "This is blood! Clearly the kings have fought together, and have killed one another. Now then, Moab, to the spoil [and the plunder of the dead soldiers]!"

But when they came to the camp of Israel, the Israelites rose up and struck the Moabites, so that they fled before them; and they went forward into the land, killing the Moabites [as they went]. They destroyed the [walls of the] cities, and each man threw a stone on every piece of good land, covering it [with stones]. And they stopped up all the springs of water and cut down all the good trees, until they left nothing in Kir-hareseth [Moab's capital city] but its stones. Then the [stone] slingers surrounded the city and destroyed it.

When the king of Moab saw that the battle was too fierce for him, he took with him seven hundred swordsmen to break through to the king of Edom; but they could not. Then the king of Moab took his eldest son, who was to reign in his place, and offered him [publicly] as a burnt offering [to Chemosh] on the [city] wall [horrifying everyone]. And there was great wrath against Israel, and Israel's allies [Judah and Edom] withdrew from King Jehoram and returned to their own land.

TRIGGERED CURSES

Triggered curses often have situational or time-based conditions attached to their activation. These curses may remain dormant for years or even generations until a specific circumstance occurs that triggers them into activity. For example, many curses within organizations like the Masonic Lodge are not activated until a particular generation fails to fulfill its obligations. If that curse is not broken in Christ, it can become active and will often lead to destruction or demonization.

Recently, I ministered to a young man who was a veteran of the Iraq war. He had survived an IED explosion, but one of his close friends tragically died in the incident. Following this, he was diagnosed with PTSD and faced numerous struggles. Despite efforts from professionals in various fields, he found little relief from his symptoms. When I sat down with him, I did not start with the presenting issue of PTSD. Instead, I focused on his ancestry and life history as I was looking for open doors or any evidence of a curse.

During our discovery process, he shared a significant event from his high school years. As a teenager, he struggled with severe weight issues and received little attention from girls, except for a set of twin sisters who began showing interest in him. They eventually invited him to their house where they engaged in sexual activities together. For a time, he believed he was living his dream life. However, during one of their visits, as the encounter reached its height, the twins suddenly stopped and presented him with a scroll. They told him that if he wanted to continue these sexual activities, he needed to sign his name on the scroll.

He explained that the scroll contained a covenant in which he agreed to offer his firstborn child to Moloch. At the time, he did not take the situation seriously and signed it without much thought. Years later, when his partner was pregnant with their first child, the curse was triggered. As she was driving over railroad tracks with their baby, the car stalled and was struck by a train thus resulting in the loss of their child. It was at this devastating moment that he remembered signing the covenant and offering his firstborn to Moloch.

This testimony powerfully reveals the reality of triggered curses tied to specific times or circumstances. In this incident, the curse served as the mechanism that brought about destruction and demonization, but its true power was rooted in the shame of what he had done. Shame kept him bound for years, which is why I was the first person he had ever trusted to confess this situation to. Yet, in His faithfulness, Jesus still brought healing, freedom, and complete restoration to his life.

SELF-IMPOSED CURSES

Our own words and beliefs can create alignments with the enemy's lies and enact curses, either over ourselves or others. Words carry power, as Scripture repeatedly emphasizes. In Matthew 12:34-37, Jesus warns, "*For the mouth speaks from that which fills the heart...But I tell you that for every careless word that people speak, they will give an account of it on the day of judgment.*" Words spoken in pain, anger, or ignorance can act as agreements with the enemy, giving him a foothold in our lives. A striking biblical example of this is found in Matthew 27:25, where the crowd, in their rejection of Jesus, proclaimed over themselves, "*His blood shall be on us and on our children!*" This self-curse, spoken in ignorance and defiance, demonstrated how words spoken in rebellion or under the influence of evil can result in far-reaching consequences.

Sometimes, the words we speak over ourselves in moments of despair, hurt, or frustration act as agreements with the enemy and establish strongholds. These internal vows or declarations are often made in response to deep emotional wounds, but they can result in unintended spiritual bondage. Statements such as, "I will die before telling what I have done!" establish secrecy and fear, further allowing shame and guilt to grow unchecked. Words like, "If it hurts that much, I will never love again!" close the door to relationships and emotional healing and align the individual with bitterness, isolation, and fear. Declarations such as, "I wish I was dead!" invite a spirit of death and destruction into a person's life further perpetuating hopelessness and despair. Words carry the power of life and death and ultimately, shape our realities and align us with either God's truth or the enemy's lies. Understanding this power is crucial to recognizing the spiritual consequences of the words we speak.

GENERATIONAL CURSES

A generational curse is any curse, no matter the type, that is passed from one generation to the next generation. Now, when many people reference generational curses, they are actually referencing the curse of sin or the curses attached to the Old Covenant law. However, when I use that term, I am speaking about any curse that is actually passed down from generation to generation. At this point, I want to deviate from many of my friends and acquaintances who reference the passages out of Exodus 20 in relation to current generational curses. Exodus 20:4-6 says this:

> *You shall not make for yourself an idol, or any likeness of what is in heaven above or on the earth beneath, or in the water under the earth. You shall not worship them nor serve them; for I, the Lord your God, am a jealous God, inflicting the punishment of the fathers on the children, on the third*

> *and the fourth generations of those who hate Me, but showing favor to thousands, to those who love Me and keep My commandments.*

Once again I believe this passage was dealt with when Christ established the New Covenant. Further, I do not believe it is appropriate for us to reference this when we are actually talking about a different type of generational curse.

When I reference generational curses, I am talking about the other types of curses, not necessarily the curse of sin or the curses related to the Law. The curses that I am referencing are when individuals come into agreement with literal demons, knowingly or unknowingly, and release a curse against a bloodline, an individual, or a group of people that continues down the generations until someone breaks it in the authority of Christ. Still, as stated before, curses are not automatically broken and must be addressed intentionally and specifically.

FUNCTION OF CURSE FROM GENERATION TO GENERATION

For curses to go from generation to generation, there are two conditions that must be established. The first condition is that an actual curse must be enacted. This can be any of the types of curses that we have mentioned in the previous sections. This activation typically takes place when an ancestor comes into agreement with a demon thus releasing an assignment against a bloodline or a family.

The second thing that must be established is a present-day permission granted through sin, trauma, or agreement with an enemy that gives place for the curse to land. Once again, just because a curse is activated does not mean that the curse has a place to land upon another individual or a family. There is a strong correlation between curses and demonization. Without curse-breaking, there will not be a lasting, effective ministry of deliverance. These two things must accompany each other.

CHAPTER 8

BRIEF DEMONIC INTERROGATION

During my 26 years of deliverance ministry, I have explored and utilized a variety of methodologies to bring about freedom for individuals. Many authors in this field take a highly dogmatic stance by insisting on a single approach to dealing with demons. While I celebrate anyone effectively setting people free through the power and authority of Jesus Christ, my experience has shown that different methods can yield better results depending on the situation.

For example, when a demon manifests and does not have a legal right to remain, you can simply cast it out in the name of Jesus, and the matter is resolved. However, if the demon does have a legal right, perhaps due to an unresolved agreement with sin, a curse, or an issue like unforgiveness, your authority in Jesus's name alone will not suffice. The person's will, being in agreement with the demon, grants it the legal right to stay. This requires addressing the root cause before true deliverance can occur.

As stated previously, early in my ministry, I adhered to a strict, dogmatic approach that avoided any engagement with demons beyond commanding them to leave. At that time, I saw approximately 60 percent of those I ministered to experience freedom. However, I was heartbroken over the remaining 40 percent whom

I could not help, despite all of my best efforts. Over time, I began to recognize a consistent pattern: the cases that resisted deliverance typically involved occult-level demons. These high-ranking demons were often anchored by generational curses or long-standing agreements and had deeply embedded themselves in the bloodline. These demons required a different approach to be exposed and expelled.

This realization led me to incorporate brief, strategic interrogations of demons during deliverance sessions. By commanding them to reveal their name, function, and legal right to remain, I gained the spiritual intelligence necessary to dismantle their strongholds. With this approach, I began to see breakthroughs in even the most resistant cases. These interrogations are not for curiosity or sensationalism, but they serve only as a tool to identify and address the hidden agreements allowing the demon to stay. While I remain cautious and deliberate in my use of demonic interrogation, I cannot deny its effectiveness. Many ministers I have spoken with, even some who were reluctant to admit it, encounter situations where they are unable to make progress in setting someone free. In such cases, a brief interrogation has often yielded profound results by uncovering the hidden legal rights and strongholds that need to be addressed.

I do not advocate for a dogmatic approach to any single methodology but do emphasize the importance of discernment and reliance on the Holy Spirit. Ultimately, the goal is always the same: to bring freedom and restoration to those in bondage through the power and authority of Jesus Christ. In the next chapter, I will break down the 15-step deliverance process that we utilize. As part of our approach, we train all our ministers to conduct a brief demonic interrogation during the deliverance session. While

I will provide a more detailed explanation later, here is an outline of the basic process for this interrogation. These questions are not for curiosity but solely to gain the spiritual intelligence needed to lead the individual to freedom while operating in alignment with the Holy Spirit's guidance.

FINDING THE NAME OR FUNCTION

When the time comes for confrontation leading to exorcism, the first step is to identify the demon by name or at least, understand its specific function within the person's life. Identifying the demon's name often provides insight into the category it falls within. For example, if the demon identifies itself as "Anger," you know you are dealing with a sin-based category of demons which tends to be lower-ranking. If it declares its name to be "Grief," it likely belongs to the trauma category. In these cases, you would proceed by commanding the demon to reveal its "boss" or the strongman of its kingdom.

During a demonic interrogation, it is critical to remain in full authority and only acting under the guidance and power of the Holy Spirit. Demons inherently seek to deceive so the interrogation must be controlled and concise. They are not permitted to speak or provide information outside of what is specifically command. If a demon attempts to disobey, I will respond decisively saying something like, "I loose the judgment of God against you," or "I strike you with the judgment of God and command you to speak only what I permit. Lie not to the Holy Spirit, or further judgment will fall upon you." This enforces the spiritual authority given to us in Christ and ensures the process remains focused.

For those who may feel uncomfortable or inexperienced in exercising the authority to loose judgment against demons, Matthew 18:18 provides further clarity and encouragement. In this passage, Jesus declares: "*Truly I say to you, whatever you bind on earth shall be bound in heaven; and whatever you loose on earth shall be loosed in heaven.*" This clearly establishes the authority given to believers to act in alignment with the will of heaven. Additionally, Psalm 149:6-9 speaks of the divine authority granted to God's people to execute judgment:

> *The high praises of God shall be in their mouths, and a two-edged sword in their hands, to execute vengeance on the nations, and punishment on the peoples, to bind their kings with chains, and their dignitaries with shackles of iron, to execute against them the judgment written. This is an honor for all His godly ones. Praise the Lord!*

Lower-ranking demons, such as those in the sin-based or trauma categories, often resist revealing the higher-ranking demon or strongman above them. Perseverance is key here. It is rare for a single demon to operate in isolation; almost always, multiple demons are present within a person. In many cases, there will be an occult-level demon at the top of the hierarchical kingdom established within the individual. While not universal, in my personal experience, over 90 percent of cases have a proper-named demon that sits at the top of this hierarchy. Identifying this top-level demon is critical before beginning the process of casting out spirits.

By identifying an occult-level demon such as "Odin," "Ra," or "Quetzalcoatl," this reveals significant spiritual intelligence about the person's demonization and potential generational ties.

For example, if "Odin" is revealed, it is likely that there is a European or Nordic demonic structure within the person. With Odin present, there is a strong likelihood that other spirits in the same kingdom, such as "Thor," "Loki," or "Freya," may also be present. Identifying the top-level demon allows you to address the hierarchical structure comprehensively. When it is time to cast out the spirits, you can command the occult-level demon to bind its entire kingdom to itself. This ensures that when the top-level demon is expelled, the entire kingdom goes with it, which saves significant time and effort by avoiding the need to cast out demons one by one. This approach is not only efficient but also ensures the deliverance is thorough and complete.

Some time ago, I led a complex deliverance session for a young woman seeking assistance. The first demon to manifest was "Anger." Upon interrogation, Anger revealed "Hatred." Hatred then revealed "Murder." Murder disclosed a connection to a human sacrifice made to "Baal." From there, Baal revealed a spirit that referred to itself as one of the "Queens of Heaven," which later identified itself as "Cleopatra." However, in essence, it was actually "Isis." Finally, Isis revealed the presence of "Osiris," a higher-ranking occult-level demon. Not all deliverance sessions follow this layered progression. Sometimes, the top-level demon reveals itself immediately, but in this case, we began at the lower-ranking spirits and worked our way up through the hierarchical structure. Once Osiris was identified, we systematically cast out all the spirits and thus, ensured the deliverance was thorough and complete.

Of course, this paragraph only took a few minutes to read, but the entire process actually took approximately three and a half hours to complete. This included detailed investigation, interrogation, and other critical steps which I will outline later in Chapter 9 as part of the 15-step deliverance process.

LEGAL RIGHT AND GENERATIONAL ROOT

When conducting deliverance ministry, it is critical to understand the legal framework of the spiritual realm and approach the process with intentionality and structure. Deliverance often resembles a courtroom proceeding where the minister enforces the laws of the Kingdom of God against demonic structures built within a person's life. Listed below is a step-by-step approach to ensure thoroughness and effectiveness during deliverance.

IDENTIFYING THE DEMON AND ITS LEGAL RIGHTS

The first step is to identify the demon by name or function and then determine whether it has a legal right to remain. Address the demon authoritatively but calmly, commanding, "Do you have a legal right to be here? Yes or no?" Always follow this with a command: "Lie not to the Holy Spirit." If the demon claims to have a legal right, it is essential to uncover the specifics such as whether this right stems from a curse, vow, sin, or unbroken agreement. For generational cases, ask how many generations it has been in the bloodline and what specific event allowed entry. For example, if a demon responds, "Murder," the next question would be, "Was this murder an act of passion, or was it a ritual sacrifice?" This distinction is vital because a ritual murder typically indicates involvement with an occult-level demon, such as Baal or Molech. Identifying the top-level demon in the hierarchical structure ensures you address the root of the issue.

BREAKING THE CURSE

Once the legal right is identified, the person must renounce the agreement. Lead them in a prayer such as this:

> *"I renounce and break the [specific curse] off my bloodline that occurred [specific generations ago]. I break this curse off my life, my family, and all my descendants, in the name of Jesus."*

As the person renounces the curse and declares the breaking of the curse over their life, continue with a prayer similar to this:

> *"By the authority of Jesus, I break this curse of [specific act] off this person, their bloodline, and their descendants. I agree with their renunciation, and I declare that this legal right is now nullified."*

VERIFYING AND BINDING

Once the curse is broken, command the demon to come forward and confirm whether it has any remaining legal rights. If necessary, repeat the process to ensure that all unresolved agreements are addressed and nullified. After confirming that no legal rights remain, compel the demon to declare:

> *"With my kingdom bound to me and having no further claims, we go now to the pit."*

EXPELLING THE DEMON

If you are ready to expel the demon, command this:

> *"With your kingdom bound to you, I command you to leave now and go to the pit."*

Some may prefer alternate destinations, such as outer darkness or judgment, but the key is to send the demon away from the person and prevent it from lingering.

If additional kingdoms are present, then command the demon to reveal any other entities: "Who else is here outside of your kingdom? Lie not to the Holy Spirit."

This step ensures thoroughness, as there may be multiple demonic structures within a person, such as a Nordic kingdom alongside a Masonic kingdom. If another kingdom is identified, repeat the process to address and dismantle its stronghold. In advanced cases, multiple kingdoms may be bound up together and expelled simultaneously, but this requires experience and a great level of spiritual authority.

FINAL EXPULSION

When all kingdoms have been addressed and all legal rights nullified, command the demons to leave:

> *"Come out, now, in Jesus's name!"*

The time required for expulsion may vary depending on the strength of the demons and the longevity of the curse. Stronger demons tied to generational curses lasting dozens of generations may resist more fiercely. Perseverance is necessary as well as a unified, team effort.

MAINTAINING AUTHORITY AND FOCUS

Throughout the process, maintain a calm and authoritative demeanor. Avoid yelling or emotional outbursts as these are unnecessary and can disrupt focus. Additionally, never seek information from a demon that is not directly relevant to the person's deliverance. Curiosity can lead to distractions and sometimes, even deception. Stay focused on the task of setting the person free.

A COMPREHENSIVE AND INTENTIONAL PROCESS

This structured approach ensures that every stronghold is dismantled, every curse is broken, and the person is fully set free in Jesus Christ. By relying on the authority of Jesus, the power of the Holy Spirit, along with sound biblical principles, deliverance ministry can bring lasting freedom and transformation.

CHAPTER 9

THE BLOODLINE DELIVERANCE AND THE 15-STEP METHOD

TRADITIONAL EVANGELISTIC MODEL OF DELIVERANCE

In recent years, God has been moving powerfully through the ministry of deliverance across the broader Body of Christ, especially in the Western church. This move is a tremendous answer to prayer for intercessors who have long carried the burden of seeing the body of Christ set free from demonization and territories liberated from spiritual strongholds. However, what we often witness on TV screens or social media only provides a partial picture of what God desires to accomplish through deliverance. Deliverance has never solely been about what we are delivered from but rather about what we are delivered into. Regardless of personal opinions, this current wave of deliverance is a manifestation of the Lord's compassion for His church. While we celebrate this great move of the Spirit, we must also acknowledge the limitations of what we see in public displays or even in our services.

Public deliverance services play a vital role in breaking open territories, both geographically and in thought. These powerful displays have challenged the mindsets of many leaders within the body of Christ and have forced dialogues in circles that were previously resistant to the ministry of deliverance. One purpose of this book is to provide healthy insights and discussion points on what deliverance should look like as it continues to grow within the church. I firmly believe that deliverance for the saints of God should be anchored in the local church without exception. This does not mean we should avoid public deliverance in the marketplace or special services; actually, far from it. I wholeheartedly affirm the value of such events.

However, the heart and primary function of deliverance ministry should remain within the local church, under the care of healthy shepherds, apostolic teams, and elders. When I refer to the "local church," I am not limiting this to the Sunday morning gathering. I am referring to the local assembly, whether in a traditional church setting, a house church, or a regional church. My emphasis is that the local community of faith should be intricately involved in the deliverance process for the individual seeking freedom.

Let me contrast some current practices in deliverance ministry. The traditional evangelistic model often involves a "special speaker" ministering to a gathering of God's people. This person preaches a powerful message, provokes demons to manifest, and finally, demons are cast out during an altar service. Thousands have been set free in these services, and I have personally led many such events over the years. They have a rightful place within the body of Christ. However, there is a danger of misrepresentation if these services are not stewarded with the local church in mind. In many public displays of deliverance, powerful manifestations occur, and indeed, demons are cast out. Yet, we must be honest: most of these individuals are not fully delivered.

What do I mean by this? Often, the specific demon manifesting is cast out, but that does not equate to complete deliverance. Demons rarely operate alone; they function in kinds or kingdoms. Celebrating a person's deliverance prematurely, without verifying that all demonic influences have been addressed, can create false assumptions. As I have learned, thorough follow-up within the local church is essential to ensuring that the person walks in full freedom. Deliverance requires an ongoing process, often involving fellowship with local elders and other spiritual leaders.

Consider Luke 8:2 which states, "*Mary who was called Magdalene, from whom seven demons had gone out.*" This passage emphasizes that seven distinct spirits were cast out of Mary. If this were simply a generalized command for demons to leave, why would scripture specify the number? Identifying demons by name or number provides clarity and further ensures thoroughness in the entire deliverance process.

When someone shares a testimony of deliverance, I often ask questions to verify the experience. For example, if someone tells me, "I cast demons out of Frank," I will follow up and ask, "How many demons did you cast out? What were their names? Did those demons have any legal rights, such as curses? Did you follow up to verify that the demons were truly gone?" Often, people cannot answer these questions. My response is, "Let's learn to be thorough. If we cannot answer these questions, we cannot confidently say the person was fully delivered." Many times, what people celebrate as deliverance is simply the cessation of a manifestation, not a verified expulsion of demons.

I recall a situation from 25 years ago when I ministered to a man for nearly seven hours. Despite intense prayer, the Holy

Spirit revealed that the man was harboring a shameful secret. When confronted, he adamantly refused to confess it and adamantly stated he would rather die than share it. The deliverance session had to be stopped, and the man left without freedom. Months later, at a special service we hosted, the man returned. People celebrated his "return to Jesus," and he fell to the floor when hands were laid on him. Sensing the unresolved issue, I quietly asked him, again, if he was ready to lay down the secret. He angrily replied, "No." The congregation celebrated his outward response, but I knew the demon remained because confession had not occurred. UPDATE: During the writing of this book, this same man actually connected with a dear friend of mine. He confessed the secret, and now, he has been fully delivered! This experience underscores the importance of honesty and authenticity in deliverance ministry.

Identifying demons by name is also crucial for accountability. If the same person returns for deliverance, knowing the names of demons that were previously cast out greatly helps discern whether the current manifestations are a new spirit or one that remained. Without such clarity, we risk operating in confusion or assumption. Luke 8:2 clearly states that Jesus cast out seven demons from Mary further demonstrating the importance of identifying each one.

This also highlights the vital role of the local church in deliverance. At The Well, we walk with individuals through their deliverance journey, often seeing them every week. We cannot assume freedom; instead, we verify and document the process. These individuals are our family, friends, and fellow believers; their deliverance requires thorough, intentional care. Deliverance is not just a ministry event: it is a community walking together into full freedom with each other. Let us commit to honesty, authenticity, and thoroughness as we walk with others into full freedom.

A REPRODUCIBLE PROCESS

Apostles and apostolic teams are the catalysts who break open new ground, both geographically and in thought. They lay doctrinal and experiential foundations further imparting understanding to the saints of God. Their role is to steward the process and speak into it, but ultimately, the ministry is entrusted to the saints.[148] Deliverance is no exception to this principle.

One of the reasons we named this methodology *Bloodline Deliverance* was to provide a clear label under which a structured process could exist. This methodology enables the ability to reproduce, a key aspect of discipleship. When settling on the name *Bloodline Deliverance*, I wrestled with calling it *The Discipleship Process of Deliverance* because discipleship is a foundational principle of all ministry within the body of Christ. Through this process, we aimed to lay a foundation of understanding for *Bloodline Deliverance* and offer a reproducible approach to guide individuals through it. However, this in no way replaces the leadership of the Holy Spirit. I cannot emphasize enough that the Holy Spirit must remain the ultimate leader in all forms and methods of deliverance ministry.

Several years ago, when this level of deliverance ministry broke out at our local church, The Well, we began multiplying teams. One of the teachers on our apostolic team came to me and said, "Mike, we need you to write out what you do because we do not understand everything that is in your mind." At the time, I had been modeling deliverance for the teams, but we did not have a written methodology or a structured process recorded. The first documentation we created came when a teacher on our team observed me walking several people through the deliverance process and documented everything. This became our first systematic approach to deliverance. Since then, it has undergone several revisions, and I have refined it further in my book, *The Self-Deliverance Guide*.

The 15-step *Bloodline Deliverance* process is the approach that we use when scheduling private or semi-private sessions. Each session typically begins with a three-hour plan. On average, this allows time to build a connection with the person, establish trust, spend time in prayer, and walk them through the process. Of course, some cases are more complex, and follow-up sessions may be necessary. Each individual is unique, coming from different backgrounds and circumstances.

This structured process differs significantly from deliverance conducted during an altar service. In altar ministry, time constraints often prevent a full deliverance process. Typically, the individual comes forward already manifesting a demon. In such cases, we focus on dealing with the manifested demon or its kingdom but rarely proceed to a full deliverance. Attempting complete deliverance without an interview or understanding the person's background is extremely challenging. Altar services are also where demons may attempt to pull you into a premature exorcism as they know they still have legal rights or powerful curses to fight from.

We have also learned that just because a demon manifests does not mean that it is the timing of the Lord to cast it out. We do not allow demons to set our schedule or agenda. Likewise, we also do not let someone else's crisis become our crisis. We are led by the Holy Spirit, who guides us into all truth, not by manipulation or fear. Over the last year, we have conducted over 1,400 deliverances through our local apostolic center. Because of the high demand, we have created systems to schedule our leaders and teams. While we are compassionate toward people facing legitimate crises, we do not let fear or urgency dictate our process. We have systems in place, and outside of a direct word from the Lord, we adhere to those systems.

It is essential to honor the time and commitment of all team leaders and volunteers. If you constantly ask for extra commitments or exceed agreed-upon timeframes, it will greatly risk burning out the team and thus, losing their support. A structured approach ensures both the needs of the people requesting deliverance and the sustainability of the teams are balanced effectively.

THE 15-STEP BLOODLINE DELIVERANCE PROCESS

1. Interview
2. Opening Declaration and Dividing of Soul and Evil Spirits
3. General and Specific Curse-Breaking
4. Renouncing Occult/Cults
5. Renouncing Soul, Sexual, and Emotional Ties
6. Renouncing Fear/Nightmares
7. Forgiveness (Inner Healing)
8. Renouncing Self-Harm and Suicide
9. Breaking Attachments to Tattoos
10. Declarations of Agreement
11. Brief Demonic Interrogation
12. Bind Their Kingdom Together
13. Lift Any Curses—Cast Them Out!

14. Check and Recheck
15. Release Generational Blessing

1. INTERVIEW

There are several key aspects and goals for the interview process in deliverance ministry. Ideally, the person you are sitting down with should have already completed intake paperwork, which you should review beforehand. This paperwork provides insights into the person's background, situations they have been involved in, possible legal rights, and indications of curses. Reviewing this information can help you discern whether the deliverance will be a more complex case or a relatively straightforward one. Based on this, you may decide to schedule more or fewer intercessors, which is a decision that becomes easier with experience.

Among the many goals of the interview, two primary ones stand out: connection and revelation. Building a connection with the individual is critical, especially since the person coming in may already feel anxious or uncertain about this process. After all, most people are not exactly excited about dealing with demons. Establishing a connection sets the person at ease and fosters trust so they feel safe enough to share some of the most painful and personal experiences of their life. Often, people will reveal things to you that they have never told another living soul; this carries a great weight of responsibility. Be prepared for the magnitude of what you might hear.

During the interview, introduce the person to your team. Share a bit about yourself and your experience with deliverance ministry. If this happens to be your first deliverance, be honest, and let them know. Reassure them that the process is not just about you or the team; it is about working together to uncover God's revelation and invite His power and presence to bring freedom. This is not about you being an "expert." Instead, it is about being a trustworthy friend walking alongside them on their journey to freedom.

Explain how the process will unfold. Let them know that you will be asking a lot of questions and may ask for details but might also redirect the discussion to another topic, especially if time is limited. Some people may have been in counseling for years and are accustomed to lengthy conversations about their emotions or issues. Setting this expectation early allows you to manage the conversation without appearing rude or uncaring if you interrupt or shift the discussion. Additionally, demons often use a tactic of encouraging excessive talking without providing meaningful information. You must discern this, and keep the conversation focused on important matters.

During the interview, focus on identifying primary open doors and observing patterns that may reveal the presence of demons or curses. One essential question that I always ask early on is, "Do you believe you have a demon?" If they answer yes, follow up by asking if they know how the demon entered, whether they know its name, or if they have interacted with it. Ask if they have seen the demon in dreams or if it has manifested in the natural realm. This helps to understand their perception of the demonic presence. It is shocking how many times someone can give you specific details to these questions which saves a lot of time during the discovery process.

It is also important to ask about family history, including their mother, father, and grandparents on both sides of the bloodline. Be attentive to any legends or family folklore passed down through the generations. Even if they are unsure of the truth behind these stories, such details can provide leads for prayer as legends often have a kernel of truth, even if embellished over time.

During the interview process, it is also crucial to not only focus on the person's ancestry but also reference their intake form to discuss potential legal rights that they may have granted to demons through specific sins in their life. For example, you should ask about potential soul ties and sexual connections. I typically request the first name of every person they have been with sexually and make a list to address later during the process of breaking those legal rights. Additionally, inquire about any involvement in the occult or any cultic rituals. This includes any activities or practices that they may have participated in, knowingly or unknowingly. It is also essential to identify whether the person is harboring bitterness or unforgiveness toward others. Compile a list of individuals they need to forgive to address these legal rights later in the process.

Further questions should cover any acts of rebellion, murders, or violence that they may have committed or have been involved in. These actions often provide significant legal rights for demonic oppression. Finally, ask them if there are any other issues or details that need to be addressed. This open-ended question often reveals areas that they might not have initially considered or remembered and further ensures a comprehensive approach to their deliverance. In summary, the interview process is about connecting with the individual, building trust, gathering critical information, identifying open doors, and recognizing patterns within the family that might reveal curses or areas requiring deliverance.

2. OPENING DECLARATION AND DIVIDING OF SOUL AND EVIL SPIRITS

As you transition from the interview process to the opening declarations and issuing specific commands, it is important to establish control from the outset. If the demon manifests before you are ready to command it forward, immediately bind it and command it to go down and remain silent. Demons often attempt to manifest early to pull you into a premature battle while they still have a legal right or an unbroken curse empowering them. The goal is to remove all legal rights and break all curses before forcing the demon to manifest and reveal its name or other necessary information. Do not let the demon dictate the process; this phase is about ministering to the person, uncovering revelations, and setting the order for what is to come.

OPENING DECLARATION

I have the person declare this: "I command all parts of my mind to be in submission to my will, which is to know the Lord Jesus, to walk with Him, and to follow His ways." The purpose of this declaration is to establish and proclaim the person's will to follow Jesus openly. This can save valuable time later, particularly if you encounter split personalities or alternate parts with conflicting loyalties. By making this declaration, the person is establishing their core will and desire to know and follow Jesus which can be referenced later as a foundational statement during the deliverance process.

Often, during this time, I ask the person if they are okay with me anointing them with oil. While not a requirement, anointing with oil is a traditional practice in the church, and I find it helpful in creating an atmosphere of peace and blessing. I anoint them, lay hands on them, and declare blessings and the comfort of the Holy Spirit over them.

I also inform the person to let me know immediately if they begin to feel uneasy, experience pain in their body, or notice wild or accusing thoughts in their mind. I assure them that it is okay to interrupt me, even while I am speaking or praying, and for them to share what they are experiencing. Without this instruction, people often wrestle internally with what the demon is doing in their minds and become distracted. Once these thoughts are brought into the open, they typically lose their power and influence. If necessary, I pray over the person, commanding the demons to be silent, stop confusing their mind, and remain bound until called forth for judgment.

ESTABLISHING EYE CONTACT

I ask the person to look me directly in the eyes. While this may feel uncomfortable, it is an important part of the process. It is not uncommon to see the presence of a demon manifest in their eyes before any physical manifestations occur. At this point, I lift my Bible as a prophetic act, move it downward, and issue the following command:

> *"In Jesus's name, I command a separation of soul and evil spirits. I command all demons to separate from their mind and body right now. I command you to retract all your tentacles from their life, in Jesus's name."*

One time, I recall issuing this command during a high-level deliverance for a man who had been suffering from tinnitus caused by an explosion during his military service. For years, the constant ringing in his ears had tormented him. As soon as I issued this command, the tinnitus instantly disappeared. The man leapt from his seat, hugged me, and thanked me profusely. Of course, I pointed him to Jesus. This miraculous moment confirmed that the symptom had been caused by a demon, and the healing came as the demon was commanded to retract.

SETTING THE TONE WITH ADDITIONAL COMMANDS

Your opening declaration and the separation command are powerful steps in the deliverance process as these further establish authority over the demons. At this stage, I issue additional commands to set the tone for the session:

> *"Demons, you will not manifest outwardly with shows of violence. You will do what you are commanded at all times. You will not speak unless I explicitly command you to speak, and even then, you will only say what I command. Should you disobey these commands given in the name of Jesus Christ, I will strike you with the judgment of God, and you will come under torment until you obey fully. Furthermore, demons, I command you now to receive the judgment and wrath of Almighty God for what you have done to this person and their family. You will remain under torment and judgment until the time I call you forth."*

By issuing these commands, the tone and authority are established for the deliverance process. Remember, demons have wills of their own, and they will test you to see if you will follow through in your authority. It is critical to remain firm and consistent throughout.

3. GENERAL AND SPECIFIC CURSE-BREAKING

In my book *The Self Deliverance Guide*, available on Amazon or my website MikeBrewer.life, I include several pages of curse-breaking declarations. These declarations begin broadly and address ancestral witchcraft and false religions. However, they also include more specific renunciations for curses related to rejection, abandonment, rebellion, and other areas. These are designed to address both ancestral curses and self-imposed curses that the individual may have spoken over themselves.

After leading someone through general curse-breaking, then transition to specific curse-breaking. This step involves using the information gathered during the interview process to address particular open doors in the person's ancestry. For example, while general curse-breaking may include renouncing any murders committed by ancestors, specific curse-breaking will involve renouncing a known act, such as a great-grandfather committing murder. The distinction between general and specific curse-breaking lies in how detailed and personalized the renunciations are and utilize the information provided during the interview.

Some of the strongest resistance that we encounter in the deliverance process occurs during curse-breaking. The more experience you gain, the clearer it will become that demons prioritize keeping curses intact. They will fight to maintain these legal rights. I have had demons manifest and plead, saying things like, "We will leave this person and never touch them again if you let us keep our curse." My response is always firm: "I strike you with judgment. You are not permitted to speak unless commanded." I do not negotiate with demons. Any uncommanded speech is met with judgment.

The more thorough and specific the curse-breaking declarations are, the more effective the process will be. I often spend 40 minutes or more on this part of the deliverance. It is critical work that significantly eases the process of dealing directly with demons later. Skipping this step will almost certainly lead to complications.

Additionally, I do not have the person read the declarations themselves. Instead, I lead them through each section of the curse-breaking manual while maintaining eye contact. This approach serves several purposes:

1. Real-time awareness: By leading them myself, I can observe exactly where we are in the process. If the person begins to manifest or show resistance during a particular section, it often reveals a legal right or a specific curse being addressed.
2. Minimizing distraction: Having the person focus on reading aloud can become a distraction. By guiding them, I help them concentrate on the spiritual significance of the moment rather than the mechanics of reading.
3. Addressing insecurities: Some individuals feel self-conscious about reading aloud, especially in front of others. Leading them ensures they remain comfortable and fully engaged.

By staying attentive and thorough during this phase, the stage will be set for a much smoother deliverance process.

4. RENOUNCING OCCULT/CULTS

This section focuses on addressing the legal rights a person may have granted to demons, either through their own actions or actions done to them. This is a crucial step in the deliverance process as unaddressed agreements or acts can serve as open doors for demonic entry and influence. For example, if a person has engaged with occult practices, such as using a Ouija board, participating in parlor games like "light as a feather," consulting psychics, conducting séances, speaking with mediums, or even playing with a Magic 8 Ball, each of these actions needs to be specifically listed and renounced. More severe involvement, such as participation in witchcraft rituals, Satanism, or other occult activities, also requires careful identification and renunciation.

In addition to occult practices, involvement with cults or false religions must also be addressed. This includes memberships or initiations into organizations such as Mormonism, Jehovah's Witnesses, Hinduism, Buddhism, or other systems of belief that oppose the Gospel of Jesus Christ. Specific rituals like baptisms, dedications, or any symbolic acts within these groups must be renounced in detail. If the person was born into a pagan or non-Christian religion, and their parents dedicated them or sought blessings from spiritual leaders, priests, or gurus on their behalf, these acts constitute a form of dedication to false gods. These dedications must also be renounced as they represent agreements made on behalf of the individual, often without their consent.

Membership in gangs, whether prison gangs, street gangs, or other organizations with ritualistic practices, needs to be addressed here as well. Initiations, rituals, pledges, or oaths made within these groups should be treated with the same seriousness as any witchcraft ritual. Tattoos or symbols associated with such groups may also require renunciation if they were part of a spiritual dedication or agreement.

The range of possible actions and agreements that could serve as legal rights is vast and often deeply personal. Therefore, thorough questioning during the interview process is essential to uncover and address these areas. For the renunciation itself, simplicity and specificity are key. For example, if the person participated in witchcraft and offered their blood in a ritual to a specific spirit, you would have them declare something like:

> *"In Jesus's name, I renounce offering my blood to [name of the spirit]. In Jesus's name, I break all agreements and revoke this act."*

This structured approach ensures that all open doors are addressed, renounced, and sealed in the authority of Jesus's name and sets the stage for effective deliverance.

5. RENOUNCING SOUL, SEXUAL, AND EMOTIONAL TIES

This section addresses severing ungodly bonds created through sexual, emotional, or spiritual ties with other individuals. Rooted in the soulish realm, these connections must be renounced to ensure complete freedom and healing.

SEXUAL TIES

Every individual with whom the person has had sexual relations must be specifically named and renounced. This includes consensual sexual relationships as well as situations of abuse, such as sexual assault, rape, or incest. In cases of abuse, the person must renounce the connection with the abuser and, crucially, walk through forgiveness to sever all spiritual ties with that individual. If any of the sexual partners were involved in witchcraft, Satanism, or other occult practices, this must also be noted. In such cases, a more thorough renunciation is required to ensure all spiritual connections are broken, particularly if the relationships involved rituals or spiritual practices.

RITUALISTIC OR CULTIC SEXUAL TIES

In many occult or cultic practices, sexual relationships are often foundational and may be ritualistic in nature. These ties require special attention and detailed renunciation. For example, if the person was part of a group that performed sexual rituals as part of their practices, each connection must be individually renounced.

EMOTIONAL AND RELATIONAL TIES

This section is not limited to sexual connections. Emotional and relational ties to controlling or manipulative individuals, such as a domineering parent, sibling, or authority figure, must also be addressed. The person should renounce any unhealthy submission or emotional attachment to these individuals. For example, if a parent exercised control through manipulation or fear, the person would renounce the emotional bond and any submission to that control.

SPIRITUAL TIES

Spiritual submission to others, such as mediums, spiritualists, or cult leaders, must also be severed. If the person previously sought guidance from a medium or engaged in rituals with others, they must renounce the spiritual, emotional, and soulish ties formed during these interactions. This includes any agreement or connection created during ritualistic behaviors, whether conscious or unconscious.

PURPOSE OF RENUNCIATION

This part of the process is focused on breaking the spiritual connections formed through sinful behaviors or abusive relationships. For example, the person might declare:

> *"In Jesus's name, I renounce and sever all sexual, emotional, and spiritual ties with [name of person or description of relationship]. I break every bond and connection formed through this relationship and cancel its effects over my life."*

By addressing and renouncing these bonds, the person can sever the influence and connection of ungodly ties, thus allowing them to fully walk in freedom and restoration through Christ.

DIVORCED

If the person has been through a divorce, this is also the point where repentance and the severing of the spiritual covenant needs to take place before God. Without this step, they may remain spiritually bound to the covenant they created. I often guide them to pray something like this:

> *"Father, in Jesus's name, I ask for forgiveness for my broken marriage and covenant. I lay that covenant before Jesus, and I ask that His blood cover it. I renounce that covenant in Jesus's name."*

This prayer allows the person to release the spiritual ties of the broken covenant and receive healing and freedom in Christ.

6. RENOUNCING FEAR/NIGHTMARES

Fear can manifest as a natural response or as a result of a spiritual source. It can be a deeply rooted stronghold or the influence of an evil spirit that requires casting out. To help people discern between natural fear and a spiritual source, I ask questions about the object of their fear. For fear to be natural, the object of the fear must be both present and potent. This means that it has the power to cause harm. For example, if I were speaking to an audience and threw a snake into the crowd, people would have a natural reason to feel fear. However, if they discovered the snake was rubber, the truth would set them free from the fear because the object, while present, no longer poses any harm. Similarly, if a real snake were miles away, the fear would also be illogical as the threat is no longer present. In both cases, the absence of logic makes it clear that the fear is unwarranted, and truth dispels it.

Conversely, if a person is sitting alone at home, reading the Bible, and suddenly feels overwhelming fear that they are about to die, this would be an illogical fear. There is no natural cause for the feeling and therefore, suggests the need to explore whether it originates from the spiritual realm or a psychological issue. In my experience, these illogical fears are often rooted in the presence of an evil spirit. This is the stage where we begin renouncing the fears identified during the interview process. A sample prayer might be:

> *"In Jesus's name, I renounce the fear of [insert object of fear] in the name of Jesus."*

When renouncing fear, it is not merely about saying the words, but it is about confronting the fear directly. I guide people to truly consider their fear and allow themselves to feel the emotional response it evokes. While those emotions are stirred, I have them declare the renunciation. This approach is important because people can sometimes dissociate from their fear and instead, go through an intellectual process without actually addressing the demonic influence rooted in the emotional stronghold. By engaging both their emotions and the renunciation process simultaneously, we confront the fear in a way that dismantles its power and breaks its hold effectively.

This section also addresses nightmares, as they are often deeply rooted in fear. Nightmares can reveal what is occurring spiritually, either through symbolic imagery or an actual encounter during sleep. By examining recurring nightmares, particularly from childhood, we can identify the object of fear and proceed to renounce it. During the interview, I often ask about early childhood nightmares or recurring dreams involving fear. These details help identify specific areas where fear has taken root and enable a focused approach to renounce and break its influence.

7. FORGIVENESS (INNER HEALING)

The three-hour deliverance session that we guide people through is not solely focused on inner healing. While individuals often come to us seeking deliverance from demons, it can feel more comfortable for them to remain in the realm of inner healing rather than confronting the demons directly. Though some inner healing is necessary to remove legal rights for demonic presence, it is essential to move beyond inner healing and engage in direct confrontation with any demons that may be present.

I have encountered people who have spent years undergoing inner healing, only to find that significant deliverance was still needed. In these cases, multiple demons were cast out during our sessions. While inner healing is effective to a degree, it cannot fully address the root issues when evil spirits remain in a person's life and must be expelled. This is not to say that inner healing is not vital as it absolutely is. We include it as part of our process but only to the extent necessary to remove legal rights. Once that is accomplished, we proceed with deliverance to remove the demons. Afterward, we connect individuals with our inner healing teams to continue walking them through restoration and renewal.

Inner healing work in deliverance sessions typically centers on broken relationships and the forgiveness required to address them. Unforgiveness creates a legal right for demons to remain. Therefore, we must carefully lead people through a list of individuals they need to forgive. However, this forgiveness must come from a deep engagement with the emotions tied to the pain caused by the other person. We do not allow people to disassociate from the painful memories or go through an intellectual exercise of simply reciting words. Forgiveness requires facing the emotional pain and choosing to release the offender despite those feelings. Here is an example prayer we often use during this process:

> *"Lord Jesus, I choose to forgive [insert person's name] for [specific actions they did]. Although they made me feel [describe emotions caused by their actions], I release them to You. Lord, I pray that they would encounter You, be restored to You, and that You would bless them."*

It is crucial for individuals to fully embrace the negative emotions tied to their experiences during this process and forgive from that place of pain. Only then can the forgiveness be genuine and deeply effective in breaking the hold of unforgiveness and any associated legal rights.

8. RENOUNCING SELF-HARM AND SUICIDE

During the interview process, there should have been an in-depth discussion about self-harm, suicidal tendencies, or attempts of suicide. It is important to document all acts of self-harm such as cutting, biting, banging their head against the wall, pinching or scratching, and any other incidents they shared. Additionally, detail any suicide attempts including the methods used such as hanging, cutting, stabbing, or the use of a firearm.

When praying through acts of self-harm, it is crucial to gather information about the emotions they felt, the compulsions they experienced, and the exact thoughts in their mind leading up to these actions. Pay particular attention to the specific phrases they may have heard internally. Often, these thoughts are not framed as, "I want to kill myself," but rather as an external directive, such as "You should kill yourself." This distinction is significant because it indicates the influence of another entity, not their own inner voice. Pointing this out can often be a moment of revelation for the individual. When renouncing these influences, have them address the voice directly, saying:

> *"I renounce you, the one that was speaking to me and trying to get me to hurt myself. I cut you off from my life in Jesus's name."*

If their self-harm involved releasing blood, it is especially important to renounce any blood covenant or appeasement offering made, whether knowingly or unknowingly, to evil spirits. Many people who engage in cutting or similar acts report experiencing temporary relief from emotional torment after the act. However, this relief is fleeting, lasting only hours, days, or weeks, until the torment returns and compels them to harm themselves again. This pattern mimics the appeasement offerings made to evil spirits or ancestors in some cultural practices. Even if the individual is unaware that they are making an offering, the act of spilling their blood can still establish such a covenant in the spiritual realm. Lead them to renounce this explicitly, saying:

> *"I renounce any blood covenant or appeasement offering I have made, knowingly or unknowingly, to an evil spirit. I break that covenant and declare it void in the name of Jesus."*

For each act or attempt of suicide, walk them through specific renunciations. It is critical to include renouncing the spirit of suicide and the spirit of death, as these demons are almost always present in cases of extreme self-harm or suicidal tendencies. For example, have them declare:

> *"I renounce the spirit of suicide and the spirit of death. I break all agreements with you in Jesus's name. You no longer have any power over me."*

Finally, guide them to make a positive declaration over themselves and affirm their identity in Christ:

> *"I declare that I am fearfully and wonderfully made in the image of God. I choose life, not death. I choose peace, not self-harm. I walk in the freedom and love of Jesus Christ."*

This process not only addresses the spiritual strongholds and agreements but also helps the individual affirm their worth and reframe their identity according to God's truth.

9. BREAKING ATTACHMENTS TO TATTOOS

I briefly referenced tattoos earlier when discussing prison gang activity and associations, but tattoos often reveal more than just affiliations. Often, they can point to specific spiritual strongholds or demonic influences. For example, if a person has multiple tattoos of the Grim Reaper, the question to ask is, "Why did you choose the symbol of death and not something like a butterfly or a rose?" In many cases, demons inhabiting the individual influenced their choice, thus drawing them to select symbols, functions, or even names that align with the demons present within them. Demons often like to express themselves subtly and embed their identity in plain sight while remaining hidden from the person's conscious awareness. Tattoos of another person's name, such as a girlfriend, parent, spouse, or a deceased friend, can also carry spiritual significance. In these cases, I often have the person lay their hand on the tattoo and declare:

> *"This tattoo is severed from any soul bonds with [name of the person]. I cut off all spiritual connections in Jesus's name, and this tattoo now only represents a season of time or a memory with that person."*

The purpose of this declaration is to sever any spiritual connections or submissions that the tattoo may represent. For example, a tattoo of someone's name can symbolize submission or emotional and spiritual ties to that person. This connection can become a gateway, binding the individual to the other person's spiritual climate. If the other person is involved in spiritual darkness, the tattooed individual may unknowingly become affected. Severing these spiritual connections ensures the client is no longer bound to the decisions or spiritual state of another person. People may ask whether they should get a cover-up tattoo, and I typically advise that it is not necessary. Instead, we "repurpose" the intent of the tattoo through spiritual renunciation and prayer. This transforms the tattoo into nothing more than ink on skin and devoid of spiritual significance.

I want to emphasize that I am not anti-tattoo nor am I legalistic on the matter. However, spiritual laws of connection must be addressed and severed. This includes renouncing any soul ties with the tattoo artist. When a person submits their body to a tattoo artist, they are granting that individual permission to inscribe something on their body, often using a creative gift or, in some cases, a demonic anointing. This interaction is spiritually significant and should be treated like any other instance of submitting to a psychic, medium, or spiritual guru. It is essential to renounce these ties to ensure the tattoo holds no remaining spiritual influence.

10. DECLARATIONS OF AGREEMENT

Congratulations! You have made it to step number 10 which means that the person has completed the majority of renunciations, removed legal rights, and closed spiritual doors. I take a moment here to celebrate with the client and acknowledge the hard work they have done to reach this point. I let them know that now, it is time for me to go into battle, both for them and with them. This step marks the transition to deeply severing ties with demons and dismantling their influence. At this point, demons may respond with anger, further manifestations, or attempts to hide. Be prepared for these possibilities.

Keep all your notes from the session in front of you, including every prayer the person has prayed, every renunciation they have declared, and every legal right that they have closed. These notes will serve as a guide to move into declarations of agreement and further spiritual warfare. I systematically go back through each renunciation and declaration made earlier in the session by addressing them one by one. This step reinforces and solidifies the work already completed and leaves no room for demonic footholds.

Here are some examples: If the client's ancestors were involved in witchcraft, I declare, "I break the ancestral curse of witchcraft off of you and your bloodline in Jesus's name." If they were involved in Freemasonry and have renounced it, I affirm, "I break the curse of the Masonic Lodge off of your life and your bloodline, in Jesus's name." In cases where a family member has committed murder, I declare, "I break the curse of murder off of your life and bloodline in agreement with your renunciation. By the blood of Jesus, that door is now closed." Similarly, if the person has attempted suicide, I say, "I come into agreement with your renunciation of suicide. By the blood of Jesus, I break the power of that act over your life, and I declare that door closed. All legal rights of the enemy are removed."

THE IMPORTANCE OF AGREEMENT

It is vital to come into agreement with every renunciation and declaration that the person has made. This partnership carries immense spiritual power. As Matthew 18:19 reminds us, "*Again I say to you, that if two of you agree on earth about anything that they may ask, it shall be done for them by My Father who is in heaven*." This step may take time, but it is essential to ensure every spiritual door is closed and every curse is fully broken.

EYE CONTACT AND OBSERVING THE CLIENT

During this process, I keep the person's eyes open at all times and maintain eye contact. This allows me to observe their responses and often reveals visible signs of relief. Many times, there will be a manifestation of peace and freedom on their face as curses are lifted, doors are closed, and healing begins to take hold.

THE POWER OF THIS STEP

Even if no demons are present, this process is transformative. These declarations remove curses, dismantle years of lies and deception, and usher in the freedom and peace of Christ. It is a sacred privilege to be the one appointed by Jesus to declare freedom to this person, and you may literally witness the Holy Spirit lifting burdens and bringing healing in real time. Do not rush this step. The breakthroughs that occur here set the stage for lasting deliverance and restoration.

11. BRIEF DEMONIC INTERROGATION

Refer to the section above regarding the interrogation of demons for specific guidelines that I strongly encourage you to follow. One of the most important things is to never give in to curiosity or pursue information that is not directly relevant to the person's deliverance. Doing so can lead to unnecessary complications and distractions.

Second, do not respond to demons if they attempt to provoke you by saying things like, "You're not strong enough," or "You don't have the power to put me out." Under no circumstances should you argue or engage in dialogue with them. If they speak without your command, immediately declare: "I strike you with the judgment of God," or ask the Lord Jesus to bring judgment upon them for their disobedience. Maintaining authority and focus is critical in these moments. I firmly believe that a brief and disciplined demonic interrogation often yields better results than attempting to cast out demons without gathering critical information. However, this method must be approached with strict adherence to well-established guidelines and a reliance on the Holy Spirit.

12. BIND THEIR KINGDOM TOGETHER

When we began the process of identifying the strongman behind demonic kingdoms and kinds, it brought a significant acceleration to the deliverance and freedom of the people we were ministering to. The phrase, "With my kingdom bound to me" has saved us countless of hours. By compelling demons to make such declarations before God and binding them together through authoritative proclamations, we ensure a more thorough deliverance process. This approach eliminates the need to address lower-ranking demons individually, thus saving valuable time and making the process far more effective.

13. LIFT ANY CURSES—CAST THEM OUT!

We have dedicated significant time in this writing to emphasizing the necessity of addressing various types of curses. As previously outlined, curses that remain unbroken can continue to affect generation after generation within a bloodline. When you identify specific curses and compel demons to reveal their entry points in the bloodline, it is crucial to take the next steps. First, have the demon confess before God that it lifts the curses. Then, issue a firm declaration:

> *"I break this curse off of you and your bloodline in the name of Jesus."*

It is essential not to invest the effort into uncovering a curse only to leave it intact. Be thorough by also leading the person to renounce the specifics of the curse that their forefathers or mothers succumbed to thus ensuring complete freedom and restoration. It is possible to deliver a person from a demon while leaving a curse against them intact. This is why it is essential to have the person renounce and break the curse and take a stand against it in faith. Additionally, you must compel the demon to confess before God that it is lifting the curse. This twofold approach ensures that not only is the demon cast out, but the underlying legal right—the actual curse—is also fully dismantled and leaves no room for its influence to persist.

14. CHECK AND RECHECK

Once the process has been completed and demons have been cast out along with their kingdoms, take time to allow the person to regroup and celebrate the incredible victory that Jesus has brought about in their life. Do not rush this part of the process; the person has often been through a multi-hour battle, and this may be the first time in their life that their mind is truly clear.

Many people have looked up at me immediately after a demon's departure and said, "My mind is clear, and I did not realize how loud it was until now as I hear silence for the first time." They often begin to weep and rejoice. Let them take in this moment of freedom; it is deeply significant.

After celebrating and recognizing the great work God has done, it is crucial to ensure thoroughness. We never want to diminish the person's faith or approach the situation with doubt, but it is crucial to verify that all demons have actually left. It is not uncommon for a demon to create a dramatic exit, such as causing the person to cough, yawn, or exhibit other manifestations, only to run and hide rather than actually leave.

At this point, I explain to the person: "This is an incredible moment of freedom, and I celebrate what you have just experienced. However, to ensure complete deliverance, I want to verify that all demons have truly departed." I often use a prophetic act, such as lifting my Bible and pointing it toward their feet while speaking directly to any remaining demons. I might say something like this:

> *"Demon, I command you in the name of Jesus to reveal yourself. You will not hide any longer, nor will you torment this person again. I command you to come forward now and face the judgment of God for your rebellion in remaining when you were told to leave, in Jesus's name."*

While issuing this command, I maintain firm eye contact with the person and lift the Bible as a prophetic gesture. If a demon remains, it will often manifest at this moment. If it is the same demon we have been dealing with already, I will say, "By your own confession, you have rebelled against the Lord Jesus. I ask

Him to release holy judgment upon you now," and then proceed to cast it out.

If another demon manifests, identify it by name and determine if it has any legal rights or curses still active. Continue the deliverance process as necessary. This is why obtaining the names of demons is so important as it allows you to confirm whether it is a separate demon or part of the same kingdom you have been dealing with. If the manifesting demon is part of the same kingdom, proceed to drive it out. If it belongs to a different kingdom, however, the process will need to be repeated to address this additional kingdom thoroughly. This level of care ensures the person's deliverance is complete and lasting.

15. RELEASE GENERATIONAL BLESSINGS

This step is what we have all been waiting for! This is one of the most beautiful parts of deliverance ministry and where the Holy Spirit is invited to come and fill them up. Further, the person begins to release generational blessings over their entire bloodline. It is quite possible that they are the first person in their bloodline to decree such blessings over their children and their children's children, unto a thousand generations. I have seen such joy and peace come upon people as they begin to release these blessings. Here is one example:

> *"Father, in Jesus's name, I come to you now as one who understands the need and power of receiving and releasing blessings. Thank You for setting me free, but I ask for more than my freedom. I pray that those who come after me will not endure the demonization I have had to endure. I dedicate my bloodline and descendants to You that Your blessing will flow to them and*

they may all know and receive You. As a mom/dad or future mom/dad, I bless my children, their children, and so on through all generations. I bless them with the revelation and power of Your love. I bless them with Your grace and mercy. I bless them with Your divine presence and protection. I bless them with wholeness, purity, and freedom. I declare and call them forth as Your covenant family in the Lord Jesus. I bless them with divine health, sound minds, godly relationships, strong marriages, and the ability to gain and steward wealth. I bless their ability to conceive and steward their children well. I bless their ability to learn and grow in education. I bless their ability to teach others. I bless their ability to communicate. I bless them with the ability to be influencers for good. I bless them as entrepreneurs, educators, governmental leaders, and influencers in the arts, entertainment, business, and finance sectors. I bless them as leaders in Your Church and Kingdom. I bless them to be worshipers of You, the one true God and Father of our Lord Jesus."[149]

PRACTICAL STEPS FOR MAINTAINING FREEDOM AFTER DELIVERANCE

STAY JESUS-FOCUSED

It is easy to become consumed with fighting demons or learning about spiritual warfare once reality has been discovered. However, always remember that the enemy would love nothing more than to divert your focus away from Jesus. Keep your eyes fixed on Him and cultivate a deep relationship with Christ. Frequently practice being aware of His presence and meditate on the truth that you are seated in heavenly places with Him as described in Ephesians 2:6: "*And* [God] *raised us up with Him, and seated us with Him in the heavenly places in Christ Jesus.*"

Immerse yourself in the goodness and power of Jesus rather than the tactics of the enemy. Memorizing and meditating on scriptures about His love, power, and victory can anchor your mind and spirit. Colossians 2:15 reminds us, "*When He had disarmed the rulers and authorities, He made a public display of them, having triumphed over them through Him.*" Romans 8:37 also states, "*But in all these things we overwhelmingly conquer through Him who loved us.*"

DEMONS LIE—DON'T BELIEVE EVERYTHING YOU HEAR

After a deliverance, it can be common to hear thoughts like, "I am still here," or "I'm back," even before you leave the room. Demons are liars and deceivers by nature. John 8:44 reminds us of the nature of demons:

> *You are of your father the devil, and you want to do the desires of your father. He was a murderer from the beginning, and does not stand in the truth because there is no truth in him. Whenever he tells a lie, he speaks from his own nature, because he is a liar and the father of lies.*

If a curse or right has been broken in Jesus's name, it is broken. You don't need to keep redoing the work unless new, specific details emerge. For instance, if you previously broke Freemasonry curses in general and later learned that your father participated in it, you can pray specifically for his involvement. However, do not let the enemy trap you in a cycle of doubt about the power of your words. Speak the truth of Scripture over your life and stand firm. James 4:7 says, "*Submit therefore to God. But resist the devil, and he will flee from you.*"

KEEP YOUR MIND AND RELATIONSHIPS CLEAN

Fill your mind with God's Word and other uplifting material. Make time to read the Bible, listen to worship music, study Christian books, and absorb good teaching podcasts that nourish your spirit. Avoid influences that distract or drain you spiritually. Dwell on the things that Philippians 4:8 describes: "*Finally, brothers and sisters, whatever is true, whatever is honorable, whatever is right, whatever is pure, whatever is lovely, whatever is commendable, if there is any excellence and if anything worthy of praise, think about these things.*"

In this season, consider re-evaluating relationships that pull you away from God or feed unhealthy patterns. Prioritize connections that build you up and encourage your walk with Christ. Develop habits like practicing gratitude in the morning and at bedtime, and daily, put on the armor of God to guard your mind and heart against any attacks of the enemy as described in Ephesians 6:10-18:

> *Finally, be strong in the Lord and in the strength of His might. Put on the full armor of God, so that you will be able to stand firm against the schemes of the devil. For our struggle is not against flesh and blood, but against the rulers, against the powers, against the world forces of this darkness, against the spiritual forces of wickedness in the heavenly places. Therefore, take up the full armor of God, so that you will be able to resist on the evil day, and having done everything, to stand firm. Stand firm therefore, having belted your waist with truth, and having put on the breastplate of righteousness, and having strapped on your feet the preparation of the gospel of peace; in addition to all, taking up the shield of faith with which you will be able to extinguish all the flaming arrows of the evil one. And take the helmet of*

salvation and the sword of the Spirit, which is the word of God. With every prayer and request, pray at all times in the Spirit, and with this in view, be alert with all perseverance and every request for all the saints.

COMMIT TO A CHURCH FAMILY

Being part of a Spirit-filled church is crucial. Resist the lie that you do not have time or a need to attend in person. In the digital world, it is easy to think that online church is sufficient, but this is simply not the same as being in a community of God in person. Commit to corporate worship, fellowship, and being part of a healthy church family. Hebrews 10:25 further speaks of this importance: "*Not abandoning our own meeting together, as is the habit of some people, but encouraging one another; and all the more as you see the day drawing near.*" Even if it requires sacrifice, such as driving an hour, it is worth it. Online sermons can supplement your growth but cannot replace the accountability and connection found in a local church. Give the church leadership permission to speak into your life and hold you accountable for your commitments. It may stretch you, but the benefits will far outweigh the challenges.

SHARE YOUR TESTIMONY

Sharing your story can be a powerful way to solidify your freedom and help others step into theirs. Revelation 12:11 states, "*And they overcame him because of the blood of the Lamb and because of the word of their testimony, and they did not love their life even when faced with death.*" You do not need to share every detail necessarily, but focus on glorifying God and highlighting how He delivered you. Speak about overcoming demonic assignments and breaking curses off of your life. Sharing your testimony encourages others and further reminds you of God's faithfulness. Your story may be the very key someone else needs to unlock their freedom and deliverance. By taking these steps, you will not only maintain your freedom but also grow deeper in your walk with Christ, further reflecting His light and victory to others.

CHAPTER 10

WHEN THINGS ARE NOT GOING RIGHT

Deliverance ministry is both a supernatural calling as well as an intense battle. We are waging war against entities that have rebelled against God and seek the destruction of humanity. The stakes are high, and the resistance is real. This level of conflict means you must not be surprised when obstacles arise or things do not always go as planned. Perseverance, reliance on the Holy Spirit, and unwavering faith are essential for breakthrough.

CHALLENGES DURING DELIVERANCE

While the authority of Jesus Christ ensures ultimate victory, the enemy frequently throws up roadblocks and brings significant resistance. These can come in many forms: spiritual interference, the person's own struggles, or even the weariness of your deliverance team. Addressing these challenges requires not only spiritual authority but also wisdom and patience. Let's walk through some of the kinds of challenges that you may face, how to overcome them effectively, and how to keep the session focused and productive.

LACK OF COOPERATION FROM THE PERSON

At times, the individual receiving deliverance may emotionally or mentally withdraw, creating a barrier to progress. This withdrawal could stem from fear, shame, or demonic interference trying to hinder the process. It's essential to gently encourage the person to re-engage without pushing them too hard. Pray for peace to settle over their mind and spirit, reminding them of God's love and their authority in Christ. Second Timothy 1:7 reassures us, "*For God has not given us a spirit of timidity, but of power and love and discipline.*"

FATIGUE

The person may become physically or emotionally exhausted during the session, which will make it difficult to proceed. Use discernment to identify the source. If it is from natural fatigue, consider taking a break or rescheduling the session to another day. If it is spiritual fatigue, pray against the spirit of weariness and command it to release the person. Always rely on the Holy Spirit to guide your next steps at this point in the process.

CONFUSION

Confusion often manifests when mind-control spirits are at work thus causing the person to struggle with focus or comprehension. In these situations, pause to pray for clarity and command any spirits of confusion or mind-control to be bound in Jesus's name. Use straightforward, simple instructions, and take time to help the person as they process. James 1:5 encourages us, "*But if any of you lacks wisdom, let him ask of God, who gives to all generously and without reproach, and it will be given to him.*"

UNDERSTANDING FRACTURED OR FRAGMENTED PARTS

A very common but potentially complex situation in deliverance ministry involves what is known as alters, fragmented personalities, dissociative identity disorder (DID), or multiple personality disorder (MPD). Let me emphatically state that we never attempt to diagnose psychiatric conditions. In deliverance ministry, our role is to offer prayer support grounded in our Christian faith as we believe that God can supernaturally heal and restore individuals facing these challenges. Often, when dealing with a very stubborn or resistant demon, the demon may be hiding behind a fragmented part of a person's soul.

Early in my ministry, over 26 years ago, I did not believe this was a legitimate condition. I assumed any such manifestation was merely a demon masquerading as a part of a person's soul. However, I was wrong. One day, I was ministering to a woman in her 50s and making no progress. The Holy Spirit brought to my mind a book that I had read that briefly mentioned split personality disorder. Acting on that insight, I attempted to address a part of her mind that had split off, essentially a child-like fragment stuck at a young emotional age. To my amazement, this grown woman began to display the temperament and behavior of a terrified child. By engaging with this childlike part, offering healing and reassurance, and inviting Jesus into the situation, she experienced restoration. Once healed, the demons that had previously hidden behind this wounded fragment were easily expelled.

Without proper mentoring, this phenomenon can be challenging to understand or address. I include this section so you can recognize such cases and seek mentorship if needed. We discuss this extensively in my one-year Deliverance Mentoring Community, which is accessible online at MikeBrewer.life.

If you encounter this situation, here are some essential points to keep in mind:

- It is not demonic. These fragmented parts are not demons; they are aspects of the core person's mind that have fractured due to trauma.
- The fragment often forms at the point of pain. These splits occur when a person experiences severe trauma or abuse, creating a coping mechanism for survival.
- Build trust and remove false guilt. These parts often carry shame or false guilt for what happened. Your role is to affirm their innocence and shift the blame to where it belongs—on the abusers or the demonic.
- Ask if they want healing from the pain. Engage with the fractured part directly, offering reassurance and asking if they want to be healed.
- Pray for healing. Lead them in asking Jesus to come and bring healing and comfort to that part of their soul.
- Lead them through forgiveness. Help them choose to forgive those who caused the pain, as forgiveness is key to healing.
- Discover any demons present. After healing the fractured part, you may find demons that had been hiding behind it. Once their legal rights are removed, expel them in Jesus's name.

When you identify a fragmented part, be patient and gentle. Speak to the part as though you are addressing a scared child or a wounded individual. Ask questions to build trust, such as:

- "How old are you?"
- "What happened to you?"
- "Would you like Jesus to take away your pain?"

After gaining their trust, pray with them and lead them to invite Jesus into their memories and their pain. Once they experience His healing presence, reintegration with the core person often happens by asking Jesus to restore their mind to wholeness. Finally, as the person is restored, be attentive to any lingering demonic presence. These demons, having lost their hiding place, may manifest and reveal themselves. Proceed as you would with any deliverance session: identify their name and function, remove their legal rights, and cast them out.

Ministering to fragmented parts requires discernment, patience, and a reliance on the Holy Spirit. It is a deeply compassionate work that allows people to experience healing in areas that they may have carried pain for decades. If you encounter this phenomenon and feel unprepared, do not hesitate to seek guidance from seasoned deliverance ministers. Remember, Jesus is the ultimate healer, and His love can restore even the most broken soul.

OBSTINATE DEMONS

Some demons will outright refuse to comply, even after curses and legal rights have been addressed. Ephesians 6:12 reminds us, "*For our struggle is not against flesh and blood, but against the rulers, against the powers, against the world forces of this darkness, against the spiritual forces of wickedness in the heavenly places.*" Be firm and unwavering. Enforce God's authority through clear and persistent commands. The key is consistency; do not relent until the demon submits to the name of Jesus.

DEMONIC DELAYS

Demons often attempt to delay the session, hoping to wear down the team or the individual. Stay focused on the Holy Spirit's guidance, and do not allow yourself to be drawn into unnecessary battles. Luke 10:19 reminds us, "*Behold, I have given you authority to walk on snakes and scorpions, and authority over all the power of the enemy, and nothing will injure you.*" Maintain your focus and enforce that authority.

TRANCES OR COMATOSE STATES

At times, a demon may push the person into a trance-like or seemingly lifeless state to avoid confrontation. This tactic can be disconcerting, but it is critical to remain calm and persistent. Gather your team in prayer and command the demon to release its hold. Continue interceding and declaring God's authority until the person is fully present again. For example, during one session, a woman collapsed and appeared unconscious. After verifying she was physically stable, my team and I prayed and worshiped for over an hour before she emerged from what we discerned was a demonic trance. While exhausting, perseverance in such moments is critical to achieving breakthrough.

TEAM WEARINESS

Deliverance ministry can be physically and spiritually exhausting, particularly during prolonged sessions. Team members may grow weary or distracted, which can impact the flow of the session.

Isaiah 40:31 offers encouragement during these times: "*Yet those who wait for the Lord will gain new strength; they will mount up with wings like eagles, they will run and not get tired, they will walk and not become weary.*" Encourage your team to stay rooted in prayer and take short breaks as needed to recharge.

PERSEVERANCE IN DELIVERANCE MINISTRY

When challenges arise, remember that you are not fighting in your own strength. Perseverance in deliverance ministry is about staying connected to Jesus and relying on His authority. Keep your focus on the Holy Spirit, and do not let the enemy's tactics distract or discourage you. By addressing these challenges with discernment, prayer, and confidence in Christ, you can lead individuals to the freedom and healing that Jesus provides as described in Galatians 5:1: *"It was for freedom that Christ set us free."* Every obstacle is an opportunity to demonstrate God's power and bring glory to His name.

TEAM DYNAMICS

Deliverance ministry is a calling for all believers, not just a specialized few. It operates as a vital part of the body of Christ, yet it is essential that the fivefold ministry—apostles, prophets, evangelists, pastors, and teachers—equip the saints to engage in this work effectively. While all believers should participate in deliverance ministry, leaders of apostolic hubs or churches must prioritize equipping others for this ministry, further ensuring the development and health of ministry teams over handling the day-to-day sessions themselves. Oversight from elders and fivefold ministers is vital to maintain accountability and provide guidance.

SELECTING MINISTRY TEAM MEMBERS

The process of selecting ministry team members is foundational to the success and integrity of the deliverance ministry. Some teams will handle general deliverance while others will address more complex cases requiring specialized training. While you do not need perfect Christians on your team, team members should live holy lives, be free of open sin, and maintain healthy relationships within the body of Christ. It is crucial to find trustworthy individuals who can handle sensitive information with care and confidentiality.

To ensure trust, all team members sign confidentiality agreements. This helps those seeking deliverance feel secure enough to share deeply personal and often painful experiences. Without this assurance, they may withhold critical details thus hindering their freedom.

TEAM LEADERSHIP

Team leaders are held to a higher standard of selection. These individuals must have strong communication skills, the ability to remain calm under pressure, and demonstrate effective leadership qualities. Confidence in their identity in Christ is essential as insecurity can lead to poor decision-making or disruptions in the deliverance process. Leaders must also be competent in documenting sessions and be able to articulate what was accomplished and provide this information to leadership for review and record-keeping.

A standard deliverance team consists of three members: a team leader and two assistants. The leader's role extends beyond managing the session to mentoring the assistants which will equip them to lead their own teams in the future. This mentoring process includes preparing the room and setting expectations with the team prior to the session.

ORDER AND FLOW IN DELIVERANCE SESSIONS

Deliverance sessions must follow a structured flow directed by the team leader. Assistants are encouraged to share revelations with the leader but not directly with the person receiving ministry. This ensures information is vetted before it is shared and prevents confusion or unnecessary agreements that could grant legal rights to demons. For example, an immature assistant might blurt out, "I think you have a Leviathan spirit." Even if untrue, the person receiving ministry may believe it thus potentially opening a door for demonic influence. To avoid such situations, assistants communicate privately with the team leader who discerns whether the revelation is relevant and should be spoken aloud or not. As trust develops within the team, this process can become more fluid.

BALANCING REVELATION AND FOCUS

Revelation, particularly from team members with seer gifts, must remain focused on actionable information such as legal rights, curses, or the identity of demons. Descriptions of demons' appearances, while vivid, are often irrelevant to the deliverance process. Leaders should guide the team to prioritize revelations that contribute to the session's objectives.

COMPASSION WITH DISCERNMENT

While compassion is a vital quality, it must be exercised with wisdom. Assistants with pastoral hearts may instinctively comfort the individual during intense moments, but this can interrupt the process. For instance, hugging or soothing someone during a critical breakthrough moment may pull them away from confronting their pain or the demonic stronghold. The most compassionate action is often pressing through the discomfort to secure the person's freedom. That said, there are moments when physical or emotional comfort is appropriate, but these should be directed by the team leader and not initiated by assistants. Leaders must ensure the focus remains on the deliverance process while balancing compassion with the necessity of addressing spiritual bondage.

THE ROLE OF THE TEAM LEADER

The team leader bears significant responsibility for ensuring the flow, order, and effectiveness of the session. They direct the ministry's progression, manage the team's interactions, and discern how information and actions are executed. This level of responsibility requires strong spiritual maturity, leadership skills, and a clear understanding of deliverance dynamics. By selecting, equipping, and guiding teams with these principles in mind, deliverance ministries can operate with integrity, effectiveness, and care, thus ensuring that each individual seeking freedom experiences the transformative power of Christ.

VIOLENT DEMONIC MANIFESTATIONS

It is not uncommon to witness violent demonic manifestations during deliverance sessions, and these must be handled with wisdom and care as they can escalate quickly and result in injury. Such manifestations often occur at the beginning of the session or when commanding the demon to come forth and reveal its name. As a foundational rule, do not allow any manifestations beyond what you specifically command. Demons are inherently disobedient and will often try to seize control to avoid being expelled. Before calling a demon forward, I set clear boundaries by saying something like, "You will not manifest outwardly or act violently. You will do only what I command, and if you disobey, the judgment of God will strike you." This preemptive approach establishes authority and minimizes disruptions.

If you are new to deliverance ministry or working with a young or inexperienced team, demons may test your limits to see what you will tolerate. This makes it all the more important to maintain firm authority and clear commands. Demons such as murder are among the most violent I have encountered. They can erupt with sudden and intense outbursts. To mitigate this, always position the team close to the person being ministered to, particularly during moments of confrontation. If necessary and only with prior permission from the individual, you may need to momentarily restrain the person to prevent harm to themselves or others. To ensure legal and ethical safety, our ministry requires clients to sign a liability waiver before proceeding with deliverance sessions. This waiver explicitly addresses the possibility of restraint during emergencies.

As you grow in faith and experience, employing the assistance of God's angels can effectively reduce outward manifestations of violence. Many seasoned deliverance ministers, including myself, regularly ask for angelic intervention. For example, if a demon begins to act violently, I might pray: "Lord, would You send Your angels to bind this demon? Let one angel stand on its right, another on its left, and bind its hands and feet." Astonishingly, you will often witness the person physically restrained as if unseen hands are holding them. This spiritual support has significantly decreased the intensity of manifestations in our sessions.

Additionally, setting expectations and issuing specific commands to demons, such as limiting their activity to only speaking their name and disclosing legal rights, has further minimized these outbursts. If a team finds itself in an especially complex or violent situation that surpasses its current training or comfort level, the team leader should shut the session down and reschedule it until more experienced help can be secured. This decision ensures the safety of everyone involved and maintains the integrity of the ministry process.

PRACTICAL SAFEGUARDS

At our ministry headquarters in East Tennessee, where it is common for people to carry firearms legally, we have implemented safety measures to protect everyone involved. Upon arrival, clients are asked to disarm and secure any weapons which we lock in a safe until the session concludes. Once the deliverance is complete, and the client is calm, these items are returned. Similarly, we ensure the environment is free of potential hazards. Clients are not allowed to use glass coffee cups or other items that could be turned into weapons. If the individual needs to leave the room, such as to use the restroom, team members accompany them especially if there have been violent manifestations. This precaution prevents harm to the person or others.

WISDOM OVER FEAR

I share these experiences not to instill fear but to impart wisdom. Deliverance ministry is a unique battlefield where spiritual warfare manifests in tangible ways. By being prepared and vigilant, we can address these challenges with confidence and ensure the safety of all involved. The focus must remain the ultimate goal: freedom in Christ for those seeking deliverance.

CHAPTER 11

THE ROLE OF CHRISTIANS TODAY AGAINST DEMONS

There is a distinction between deliverance ministry and exorcisms with individuals versus dealing with principalities or territorial spirits over regions and nations.[150] Bloodline deliverance begins with deliverance for the individual through casting out demons but reveals spiritual intelligence that is valuable for strategic-level warfare. When individuals begin to get free in a territory, there becomes a thrust of deliverance that affects families, which then affects communities and ultimately, entire cities, regions, and nations. However, it starts with personal freedom—your freedom.

THE SPIRITUAL BATTLE DESCRIBED IN EPHESIANS 6

THE CULTURE AT EPHESUS

Regarding spiritual warfare and deliverance ministry, it is necessary to address the belief shared by Heiser and many Christians today that spiritual warfare and casting out demons are simply unnecessary since Christ conquered all at the cross. Many Christians, like Heiser, reduce their belief down to a purely mental battle that believers fight in their minds and not something that should be engaged with on a spiritual level both individually and geographically.[151] This view is extremely passive and not aggressive against these evil powers since Christ already achieved victory over them. Even Heiser's description of warfare in Ephesians 6:10–17 appears completely absent from the demonic spiritual culture of Ephesus during the first century.

Ephesus served as the primary hub for the Temple of Artemis.[152] This cult worshiped the mother-goddess of fertility, and secret rituals and magic were rampant in this cult. Acts 19 provides a further backdrop of the spiritual climate at Ephesus and Paul's time there. Ancient legends claim that the city was founded by a mythical race of female warriors who cut off their right breasts so as not to interfere with their ability to throw javelins; they were called the "Amazons." They erected a statue of the false god, Artemis, and established an annual dance using weapons and shields.[153] The modern "Wonder Woman" movies are based off of these legends. To say that this culture was absolutely influenced by demonic powers is an understatement. There is clearly a territorial spirit in operation over this region. A brief evaluation of Ephesians 6:10–17 is necessary for further understanding.

THE STRENGTH TO STAND

This passage is often described as "the most explicit cultural war text" in all of the New Testament.[154] Paul uses warfare imagery in many of his letters, but none as developed as here.[155] The role of the church in spiritual warfare cannot be emphasized enough in this passage. In verse 10, the church is called to be "*strong in the Lord and the power of His might.*" Earlier in Ephesians, Paul describes his usage of "the power of His might" in Ephesians 1:19–20 and 3:16. Therefore, "the power of His might" is an attribute of God given to His people, not something to be attained by human merits or man-made strength. Building on verse 10, to be "strengthened by the Lord" equates to putting on the full armor of God.

To "put on" here means to actively wear all that God has provided.[156] The purpose of armor was maximum protection in field warfare or hand-to-hand combat. In the biblical context, "Armor serves as a metaphor for God's protection of the righteous."[157] The "stand" mentioned in verse 11 is repeated three more times in the following verses. This "stand" is more of an offensive stance rather than just a defensive "stand" without retreating.[158] Armor is needed due to the evil, spiritual nature of the enemy, and its ultimate purpose is to resist whatever the enemy throws, even darts of fire.

WHO ARE THE POWERS?

In Ephesians 6:12 (NRSV), Paul describes the spiritual battle at hand:

> *For our struggle is not against blood and flesh, but against* ***the rulers,*** *against* ***the authorities,*** *against* ***the cosmic* [world] *powers*** *of this present darkness, against* ***the spiritual forces of evil in the heavenly places.***

These are spiritual enemies, not natural ones. Paul is also actively engaged in this spiritual battle with the believers at Ephesus. This is a corporate battle for the church and not just for one person to fight alone. This verse is connected to Colossians 2:15 stating that Christ has already disarmed these evil powers at the cross and through His resurrection.[159] Therefore, their only power lies in what is granted to them; those who are clothed in God's armor can not only withstand them, but also, defeat them.

All four of these terms can be viewed in conjunction with the rebellious *elohim* of the Old Testament. They function in the same manner as ruling, territorial spirits. The most common term we use to describe these spirits today is *principalities*. In deliverance ministry, there is a distinction between a demon and a principality. A demon is what is cast out of individuals during ground-level warfare. A principality is a ruling, territorial spirit that influences regions and nations. These are addressed through strategic-level warfare to take back these territories for the Kingdom of God. As Mike discussed previously in Chapter 7, through the many thousands of deliverances that he has done, it is extremely rare for a principality to manifest within an individual but not impossible. Let's do a brief evaluation of each of these terms from Ephesians 6:12 to understand the list that Paul is actually describing here.

THE RULERS/PRINCIPALITIES

The "rulers" mentioned is the Greek word *arcehē,* which is often translated as "ruler" or "principality." This word is used twice in Ephesians 1:21 and 3:10; in both cases, Paul refers to a spiritual ruler of which God's authority is supreme. These rulers are described as enemies against both God and the church. Romans 8:38-39 uses this same word to describe the same principalities which cannot separate believers from the love of God:

> *For I am convinced that neither death, nor life, nor angels, nor* ***principalities****, nor things present, nor things to come, nor powers, nor height, nor depth, nor any other created thing will be able to separate us from the love of God that is in Christ Jesus our Lord.*

This Greek word also refers to "a chief" or "the first in order, time, place, or rank." Paul is also referring back to the roots of these wicked principalities that were common throughout Israel's history.

THE AUTHORITIES/POWERS

The second word, *authorities*, is the Greek word *exousia* and appears in conjunction with the "rulers" in Ephesians 1:21 and 3:10; they are also used together in Colossians 2:15. Ephesians 2:2 uses this word uniquely to provide more insight into Paul's intent:

> *In which you previously walked according to the course of this world, according to the prince of* ***the power*** *of the air, of the spirit that is now working in the sons of disobedience.*

We learn that this power is in the "air" or spirit realm and seeks to cause disobedience in people. Before Christ, humans were dead in sin, operating under these spiritual authorities. Now, in Christ, believers are alive and raised up to a heavenly position with Christ.[160]

THE WORLD POWERS

The third word in Paul's list is the Greek word *kosmokratōr* and is used for "world powers." This word is not found elsewhere in the New Testament or the Septuagint. Therefore, a brief search of other writings at this time gives further insights into this word in cultural context. In ancient Greek papyri, this word is used to generally describe the gods of Helios, Ra, Hermes, and Sarapis, as well as in an ancient Roman inscription referring to the gods of

Sarapis and Mithras.[161] Therefore, Paul's usage of this word could be a reference to Artemis and the other pagan gods prominent in Ephesus, to emphasize the evil darkness of these deities.

SPIRITUAL FORCES OF EVIL

The final power mentioned by Paul is the Greek word *pneumatikos* and is translated as "spiritual forces." This word can be used as a general designation of all demonic spirits.[162] He attaches the adjective *ponēria* to these spiritual forces to further emphasize how wicked and malicious these forces are. This list appears exhaustive to further emphasize Paul's primary point: regardless of the demonic entity, Christ is exalted over all of them, and these forces are currently in operation against the church.

PUTTING ON THE ARMOR OF GOD

Continuing with Ephesians 6:13, Paul encourages the churches to "take up" their armor both here and again in verse 16: *"Therefore, take up the full armor of God, so that you will be able to resist on the evil day, and having done everything, to stand firm."* The word for "complete armor" literally means "panoply." It is the same word Paul used previously in verse 11. The only other New Testament usage of this word is found in Luke 11:22 which provides further background.

PLUNDERING THE STRONGMAN

In Luke 11, Jesus tells a story about a strongman guarding his house and possessions. However, when a stronger man "attacks and overpowers him," that man takes away his armor and distributes it as plunder.[163] Luke 11:22 says, "*But when someone stronger than he attacks him and overpowers him, that man takes away his armor on which he had relied and distributes his plunder.*"

In the Old Testament battle stories, the armor of a defeated warrior symbolized "shame for the vanquished and honor for the victor."[164] The great King Cyrus was prophesied about in Isaiah 45:1 (NIV) to "*strip kings of their armor*," symbolizing his victory and their defeat. In context then, this warfare description involves active engagement by attacking and overpowering the strongman who is guarding the house. The *elohim* of the Old Testament were the "strongmen" of their assigned territories; Paul is using the same language to imply active warfare against these territorial powers that are still operating over regions and nations to reclaim them for the Kingdom of God.

ENGAGING IN THE BATTLE

The first step for believers to engage in this war is to become aware of this spiritual battle. It is not in the distant future but is here and now. Each piece of armor must be engaged in order to stand firm in the victory of Christ over these evil powers. While Paul was writing to the house churches across the region of Ephesus, this battle with the demonic world continues to rage in the present reality in all parts of the world. This war is not against people but against the demons and evil spirits at work within the earthly realm.

While every Christian consciously engages in this battle, it is not meant to be fought alone. The church becomes the army of God composed of many soldiers, all of whom are dressed in the armor of God and ready to fight. Those outside the church's community are fighting alone and become easy targets for the enemy. A significant component of spiritual warfare is fighting in the army of God together, as a united force. This furthers Paul's continual urge for unity within the church. Without a united army, the enemy will attempt to take out as many as he can and stop the church's mission to advance the Gospel of Christ.

THE ROLE OF THE CHURCH

The primary purpose of the church in this great spiritual war is revealed in Ephesians 3:10–11 (NIV): *"His intent was that now, through the church, the manifold wisdom of God should be made known to the rulers and authorities in the heavenly realms, according to his eternal purpose that he accomplished in Christ Jesus our Lord."* It is only through the united church that the power of God is displayed to every demonic deity and hostile god. The church is thus the enforcer of Jesus's declaration of war against every evil power and is aggressively storming the gates of hell enforcing the victory of Christ!

Resurrection power requires applying the victory over death, which is true for spiritual warfare as well as for healing, deliverance, and everything else found in the atonement of Christ. This view has sadly weakened the church against the spiritual powers that are actively seeking to destroy Christians. The agenda of the enemies of God against His people has not changed: demons want to steal, kill, and destroy.[165]

Further, these powers are not just idly sitting back and waiting for someone to fall, but they are actively seeking and pursuing God's people in order to take them out. In its simplest terms, these evil powers and demons want you and me dead. This is the urgency and tone of Paul's letter in Ephesians which cannot be dismissed. Just because Christians attempt to ignore the spiritual battle or try not to engage in it does not mean that demons stop their pursuit or go away. They must be cast out and removed from their assignments and territories through the authority of Jesus.

OTHER SCHEMES OF THE ENEMY

The apostle Paul describes other schemes of the enemy in his other writings: anger and division in Ephesians 4:27, a lack of forgiveness in 2 Corinthians 2:11, subtle schemes in 2 Corinthians 11:14, and the lack of self-control in 2 Corinthians 7:5.[166] Part of spiritual warfare involves renewing the mind and casting down speculations and deceptive thoughts.[167] These are also important parts of the overall deliverance process through discipleship.

POSSESSION OR DEMONIZATION?

A major debate in modern Christianity is this question: "Can a Christian be possessed?" Denominations and theologians are typically divided when this question is asked. However, before a conclusion can be reached, one must first look further at the actual question being asked. The term *demon-possessed* often comes from modern biblical translations in the New Testament to describe those who were manifesting a demon that resulted in it being cast out of a person. The New American Standard Bible, King James Version, New International Version, and New Revised Standard Version translations all use the English term *demon-possessed* for the Greek word, *daimonizomai*. The English Standard Version uses the phrase "oppressed by a demon."

A deeper study of this Greek word reveals a more complete understanding though. There are thirteen usages of *daimonizomai* in the New Testament. Strong's defines this verb to mean, "to be under the power, control, or influence of a demon." If the question was rephrased to say, "Can a Christian be under the power, control, or influence of a demon," the modern debate may change drastically. Most of us would agree unanimously, yes.

The English word *possession* implies ownership, occupancy, and complete control over.[168] This is not the same definition as *daimonizomai*. A born-again, Spirit-filled believer cannot be under the ownership of a demon; however, they can live influenced or tormented by it. When someone comes into salvation in Christ and has repented of their sins, they enter into the New Covenant through the blood of Jesus. However, what they did previously in their lives does not mean demons just disappear at the moment of their conversion. We choose to use the word "demonized" instead of "possessed" as this more accurately describes the meaning of *daimonizomai*.

The same principle can be applied as with sickness. All sickness is covered by the blood of Jesus through the atonement on the cross. So why do many believers still struggle with sickness? We are living in the reality of the tension of the Kingdom of God. Jesus paid for it all, but we are still walking into the fulfillment of that promise. The Kingdom of God was inaugurated at the death and resurrection of Christ, but it is still growing into full maturity, which will culminate upon the final return of Christ. We live in that tension of here and now, but not fully manifested yet.

If someone is born again and struggling with demonic torment, this does not mean that they are not saved. They are simply in the deliverance process, which includes the casting out of demons but also inner healing, renewing of the mind, discipleship, and spiritual maturity. To assume this is always an issue of one's salvation is a great error that causes people to attempt to hide their struggles rather than seek help for them. It would be the same concept as assuming someone who has a terminal illness is not saved since they are still sick.

COPING VERSUS FREEDOM

The belief that a Christian cannot be influenced by a demon has caused great turmoil within the church. Many believers are struggling with deep, internal torment and feel that they have to hide it since the religious system has told them that they "can't" be experiencing this and still be a born-again believer. The results of this often lead to deep shame and even a greater level of internal torment as they feel they now have to hide and live in secrecy. The culture of the church must change to embrace these secrets and help people through the process of true freedom.

A dear friend who is a licensed counselor told me years ago, "Coping is not freedom." I watched his counseling practice transform into a powerful deliverance ministry over the years. He shared one testimony with me that he had been counseling with a young lady for a few years, meeting two to three times each week. She had over 100 counseling sessions with him. After he witnessed the fruits and power of bloodline deliverance, he led her through three deliverance sessions. She did not need further counseling after as she had received true freedom. Freedom means healing and wholeness.

Much of the church has accepted the reality of "coping" rather than experiencing the fullness of true freedom. Let me add that I am absolutely not against counseling. I do believe it is necessary, at times, and also has a role in the deliverance process. However, if someone is dealing with a demon, it cannot be counseled but must be cast out. Counseling after deliverance is often very successful to help someone walk out their freedom.

DANGEROUS DOCTRINE

I want to share another story of how dangerous the belief that a Christian cannot be demonized can be. A young pastor was dogmatically dedicated to the doctrine that Christians cannot be demonized and was a strong cessationist. He met with Mike one day along with a few other pastors who were upset about our deliverance ministry because they did not believe it was biblical. This pastor had deep anger toward Mike during this meeting. As always, he invited these pastors to come and see for themselves what God was doing to set people free and hear the testimonies from others. This never happened.

Not long after this meeting, this pastor's wife reached out to us privately. She needed deliverance but did not want her husband to know that she had contacted us. By this point, their marriage had fallen apart, and they were now separated. He had moved on into another relationship leaving her and their children on their own. He was still pastoring through all of this. The wife went through a private deliverance session and received massive breakthrough, healing, and freedom. She wanted to reconcile with her husband, but he refused. He continued to speak out against our ministry and all forms of deliverance. Six months later, he committed suicide. This was heartbreaking and tragic.

His wife told me later that he desperately needed deliverance just like she did, but the doctrines he lived by told him he could not be saved and still be dealing with these issues. The torment was so great that he took his own life. No sin is too bad nor is your torment too severe that Jesus cannot heal and deliver you! When deliverance becomes normalized back into the modern church culture, we will see a great harvest pour in as those who are demonized can find a place to receive true freedom in Jesus without shame or secrecy.

JESUS AND THE WILDERNESS

Jesus frequently cast out demons during His earthly ministry. All three of the synoptic Gospels record the same pattern of Jesus *before* He began His earthly ministry: the ministry of John the Baptist to prepare the way for the Messiah, His birth, His baptism, and the testing in the wilderness by Satan. In Matthew and Luke, the wilderness is first mentioned concerning John the Baptist. While living in the wilderness, John becomes "strong in the Spirit" (Luke 1:80) and the Word of God comes to him there (Luke 3:2). John begins his ministry immediately after leaving the wilderness and entering the district near Jordan. Jesus is baptized by John at the Jordan River, and the Spirit descends upon Him (Luke 3:21-22). Luke breaks the narrative to give Jesus's genealogy going back to Adam, the son of God, before returning to Jesus and describing Him as now being "full of the Holy Spirit" upon His return from the Jordan (Luke 4:1).

In a similar pattern as John, Jesus is described as being led into the wilderness by the Holy Spirit and is tempted by the devil for forty days; He ate nor drank anything during this time. The devil tempted Him three specific times, to all of which Jesus responded with a passage from the Old Testament concerning the Exodus narrative. The three temptations included food, dominion, and identity. After resisting each temptation, Satan fled from Jesus "until an opportune time." Jesus immediately begins His earthly ministry after returning from the wilderness in "the power of the Spirit" (Luke 4:14a) just like John.[169] Direct connections are thus revealed between the wilderness and the Holy Spirit through the patterns of John and Jesus. With this pattern in mind, all forms of ministry must be empowered by the Holy Spirit, including deliverance.

Although there are many similarities concerning the wilderness experiences of John and Jesus, John resided in the wilderness while Jesus only spent forty days there. Forty correlates with the number of years the Israelites, led by Moses, circled the wilderness before entering the Promised Land (Josh 5:6). The purpose of this forty-year period was due to the Israelites' unfaithfulness to God and their disobedience; God punished them one year for every day the spies were sent out to scout the land of Canaan and returned doubting God's promise (Numbers 14:33-35). During this time, the Israelites were tested by God to determine what was in their hearts and if they would obey or disobey God (Deuteronomy 8:1-3). The Israelites failed their test; Judges 2:10 describes the generation proceeding Joshua who "*did not know the Lord, nor even the work which He had done for Israel.*"

Therefore, Jesus repeated the same cycle of testing in the same wilderness location, one day for every year of Israel's time there. However, Jesus passed the test thus fulfilling what Israel could not do.[170] Further, as discussed previously in Chapter 5, Jesus specifically returned to the wilderness location, which was viewed as a habitation for hostile demon-gods and evil spirits, to conquer this territory once and for all.[171] Jesus also defeated the temptations of the devil while in the wilderness to further enforce His identity as *the* Son of God.

THE MINISTRY OF JESUS

Immediately following this victory, Jesus began His earthly ministry. Among the first acts of Jesus in all three Synoptic Gospels was the casting out demons.[172] Scholar E.P. Sanders argues, "The sheer volume of evidence makes it extremely likely that Jesus actually had a reputation as an exorcist."[173] This statement challenges many modern Christian views about Jesus and His ministry. Let's briefly look at Matthew 4:24 (NRSV), which is described as "simultaneously a programmatic and summarizing statement of the ministry of Jesus":[174]

> *So his fame spread throughout all Syria, and they brought to him all the sick, those who were afflicted with various diseases and pains, people possessed by demons or having epilepsy or afflicted with paralysis, and he cured them.*

A direct connection is made through the spread of Jesus's fame from the miracles He performed, including healings and exorcisms. The testimony of Jesus will always proceed forth following public healings and deliverances; it is the power of the testimony. This is why casting out demons should sometimes be done publicly and not only privately.

This specific list in Matthew 4:24 begins with healing sickness including various diseases and pains. The Greek word for *afflicted* can also be translated as *tormented* and refers to "one who is arrested such as a prisoner."[175] In this context, sickness is like a form of torment that causes bondage. The same word used for diseases is used again in Matthew 10:1: "*Jesus summoned His twelve disciples and gave them authority over unclean spirits, to cast them out, and to heal every disease and every sickness.*" Now, it's not just Jesus who has the authority and power to heal and deliver, but also, His disciples are commanded to do the same. The implication is the same: through Jesus's name, heal and deliver *all!*

Second, Jesus healed and delivered those under the influence of demons (*daimonizomai*), having epilepsy, and afflicted with paralysis. The Greek word translated as "having epilepsy" is *selēniazomai* which literally means "moonstruck; lunatic." Its only other usage in scripture is in Matthew 17:15, which describes a man who comes to Jesus pleading for healing on behalf of his son who is frequently thrown into the fire and water by a demon, but the disciples could not cast it out of him. The implication is someone who is so severely tormented by a demon that it causes symptoms similar to epilepsy; only exorcism of the demon can produce healing as was the case in Matthew 17:15.[176] In modern terms, this could be used to describe many demonic manifestations. When these manifestations are caused by a demon, it must be cast out through exorcism just as Jesus modeled; prayer, inner healing, counseling, and other methodologies are not sufficient. The final word in this list is *paralytic* referring to a person tormented from some form of physical paralysis. No matter the need, Jesus healed and delivered them *all!*

It is important to note that when Jesus healed someone who was demonized, there was still an act of exorcism involved; the demon still had to be cast out. Many English translations often use the term *cure* in the context of someone who is demonized getting delivered as is the case in Matthew 8:28-34, 9:32-34, 12:22-24, and 15:22-28. However, this is not referring to using medicinal practices or a prayer for healing. In each of these passages, Jesus still cast out a demon which resulted in the cure of a physical illness or disease.[177] The act of exorcism resulted in physical healing. Sanders further states, "Exorcism is the most prominent type of cure in the New Testament."[178] Scripture frequently references physical healing and the exorcism of demons together as a major aspect of Jesus's earthly ministry.[179]

EXORCISM AND *EKBALLO*

There are two Greek terms used to describe demons leaving people in scripture: *exerchomai* and *ekballo*. *Exerchomai* refers to the action of a demon leaving a person but not necessarily the force of them being cast out through an exorcism; it simply refers to the departure or "going out" of the demon. *Ekballo* is a verb that means "to violently and forcefully cast out or thrust forth; to expel; to drive out; to be deprived of the power and influence."[180] The majority of the references to demons being cast out in the New Testament are from the power of *ekballo*. Demons do not simply go away because Jesus shows up; they still have to be cast out through the power and authority of God. However, scripture does reveal that when Jesus shows up, demons manifest and make themselves known. They cannot remain hidden when the power of Christ is present.

While Jesus modeled the pattern for ministry, He also commanded His believers to cast out demons just as He did. This is not a specific calling for just a few but is a command for *all* who follow Christ. In Matthew 10, Jesus commissions His disciples to go forth, preach the Gospel, cast out demons, and heal the sick. In verses 7-8, Jesus also tells them to preach saying, "*The Kingdom of Heaven has come near*" in conjunction with casting out demons, healing the sick, raising the dead, and cleansing the lepers. This is the fullness of the Gospel message that is demonstrated in both proclamation and in power, in word and in deed as Paul says (Romans 15:18-19).

Jesus further commands them, "*Freely you received, now freely give.*" There is a greater measure of faith and authority from someone who has experienced freedom to then minister it to others as they can identify with that person at a greater depth. They understand the torment and can use that to fight for the other person's freedom. If you have a testimony of freedom through deliverance, then you understand the need to minister deliverance.

Finally, in the Great Commission as recorded in Mark 16:15-18, the final words of Jesus to His disciples before His ascension were this:

> *Go into all the world and preach the gospel to all creation. The one who has believed and has been baptized will be saved; but the one who has not believed will be condemned. These signs will accompany those who have believed: in My name they will cast out demons, they will speak with new tongues; they will pick up serpents, and if they drink any deadly poison, it will not harm them; they will lay hands on the sick, and they will recover.*

Concerning this passage, scholar Jeff Oliver states, "Christ's work was complete; the church's work was only beginning. Accompanying signs would authenticate their preaching, remove hindrances, draw people to faith, ensure the gospel's effectiveness, and bring glory to God."[181] Jesus ends His time on earth with a command to His disciples to "Go" and preach the Gospel, and as a result, they will cast out demons, speak in tongues, and heal the sick. The word for "cast out" here is *ekballo*. This is the essence of the Gospel message that should naturally accompany all of those who preach it. Deliverance is not just something that we go and "do," but it should naturally accompany us in our lives as part of the Gospel message of Jesus living through us.

CHAPTER 12

DELIVERANCE AND EARLY CHURCH HISTORY

Deliverance is not a new trend nor is it something that "stopped" occurring after Christ and the apostles. Church history is well-documented with deliverance and exorcisms. This section is by no means exhaustive; it only contains some documented testimonies of deliverance that follow many of the same testimonies and experiences as *Bloodline Deliverance*. It is also meant to serve as a global reminder how much of the world views demonic entities and their active roles in the world.

FIRST CENTURY

One of Jesus's twelve disciples, Bartholomew, was documented of taking the Gospel to several nations before settling in Armenia in the first century. One of the early church fathers, Jerome, documents many stories of him directly from the Armenians:

> Bartholomew preached with such success that the heathen gods were rendered powerless.... Bartholomew did many wonderful things there including the healing of the lunatic daughter of the king, and the exposure of the emptiness of

> the king's idol, and the banishment of the demon which inhabited it....The king and many others were baptized as a result, but the priests remained hostile. The priests went to the king's brother, Astyages, who had Bartholomew arrested, beaten with clubs, flayed alive, and crucified in agony.[182]

The fruits of his time in Armenia and his martyrdom are strongly revealed in the rich Christian history of this nation. Armenia became the first nation in the world to declare Christianity as its national religion in AD 301, twelve years before Constantine. Even through the Christian genocides by Muslims in the early 1900s, 98 percent of Armenians today still claim to be followers of Christ.[183]

SECOND CENTURY

During the second century, Justin Martyr described the early church and the power of the Holy Spirit working through all Christians: "For numberless demoniacs throughout the whole world, and in your city, many of our Christian men exorcising them in the Name of Jesus Christ...have healed and do heal, rendering helpless and driving the possessing devils out of the men."[184] The second and third century Christians were known for casting out demons and healing all forms of sickness. While this was done by those who were trained as priests and bishops, it was also done by the common man. Origen of Alexandria was one of the early church fathers who is also referred to by many as the first Christian systematic theologian. He discussed frequently witnessing untrained men casting out demons through simple commands in the name of Jesus: "For by these means, we too have seen many persons freed from grievous calamities, and from distractions of mind, and madness, and countless other ills, which could not be cured neither by men nor devils."[185]

THIRD CENTURY

By the third century, Christians were described as such: "Those who lived a Spirit-guided Christian life expelled evil spirits, performed many cures, foresaw certain events, and received gifts of language, wisdom, and knowledge."[186] One of the esteemed pupils of Origen was Gregory Thaumaturgus, who became known as "Gregory the Wonderworker." After studying under Origen, he returned to his homeland in Pontus, which is modern-day Turkey. Later, he rose to the position of Bishop of Neocaesarea which was the capital of Pontus. Gregory received the name of "Wonder-worker" because of his powerful ministry: "(he) performed many miracles, healing the sick, and casting out devils even by his letters, insomuch that the pagans were no less attracted to the faith by his acts, than by his discourses."[187] The testimony of his life was that when he became bishop and began working miracles and exorcisms in the city, there were only 17 Christians present; when he died, there were only 17 people in the entire city who were not Christians yet.[188] Another early church father, Basil of Caesarea, described Gregory and his ministry:

> Where shall I rank the great Gregory, and the words uttered by him? Shall we not place among apostles and prophets a man who walked by the same Spirit as they? For by the fellow-working of the Spirit, the power which he had

over demons was tremendous, and so gifted was he with the grace of the Word... Thus, in all that he through grace accomplished, alike by word and deed, a light seemed ever to be shining, a token of the heavenly power from the unseen which followed him.[189]

FOURTH CENTURY

Between the third and fourth centuries, Christian monks began to emerge from the deserts. One such monk was Antony of Egypt. His works were recorded by another early church father, Athanasius, who was also the Bishop of Alexandria. In his work, *The Life of Antony*, Athanasius records many encounters that Antony had with demons and performing exorcisms. On one occasion, Antony was visiting with other monks on a shipping vessel. He smelled an "exceedingly unpleasant smell" which the other monks attributed to the fish and other meats on the ship. Antony knew this was demonic and not from the meat. When Antony began to speak, "a youth with an evil spirit, who had come and hidden himself in the ship, cried out. But the demon, being rebuked in the name of the Lord Jesus Christ, departed from him, and the man became whole. And all knew that the evil smell arose from the demon."[190]

On another occasion, a severely demonized young man was brought to Antony to receive deliverance by other monks. The man was eating his own feces from the severity of his demonization and was out of his mind not knowing who he was or where he was at. Antony kept him overnight in the monastery and prayed over him throughout the night. At dawn, the young man violently attacked him. The other monks were angry, but

Antony recognized that this was a demon, not the man himself. Antony rebuked the demon and commanded it to leave the man and "to go into dry places." The demon became "raging mad" but then departed from the man. Immediately, the young man came to his right mind and became whole. He knew who he was again and graciously thanked God for his freedom and Antony for his help.[191]

During the fourth century, there was a rise in Christian monks and monasteries all across the Egyptian deserts. A form of a Charismatic renewal spread from these monasteries into villages, from Egypt and later into Palestine, Judea, Syria, North Africa, and Western Europe.[192] These monasteries became like Christian training grounds for those who wanted to understand how to live a Spirit-filled life. The reports and testimonies of this era were marked by the gifts and power of the Holy Spirit: "miraculous manifestations became commonplace, including visions, appearances of light-phenomena, the granting of fertility, multiplication of food, healing, deliverance, miraculous transportations, and divine protection."[193] These monks were known for their prophetic giftings and for the power to heal all forms of sicknesses and cast out demons.

Another common distinction of these first several hundred years of church history was the fact that cessationism was not a prevailing doctrine as it is in much of the church world today. In fact, just the opposite. The commands of Jesus to His disciples continued through the power of the Holy Spirit to all believers through Acts and through the early church. One of the desert monks of the fourth century, Apollonius, recorded a personal encounter he had with a demonic spirit. A demon approached him and challenged his authority to cast out demons. He responded,

"Come now. Are not the prophets and apostles they who handed on to us their faith and their grace? Was God present then and absent now? God forbid. God is almighty, and what He can do He can always do."[194]

SIXTH CENTURY

By the sixth century, these practices and beliefs continued through the church, from the pope to the common man. Pope Gregory I, also known as Gregory the Great, led the church through an era of many great miracles, healings, and deliverances. Centuries later, during the Reformation Era, John Calvin referred to Gregory as "the last good pope."[195] Pope Gregory had a strong position that the gifts and power of the Holy Spirit were to continue working through all Christians as evidenced in scripture without ceasing. Further, he connected the necessity of miracles, casting out demons, and healing the sick for evangelistic purposes, especially to convert "the pagans and heretics, as well as for strengthening the hearts of the faithful."[196] This same principle is true today. For those who are actively practicing witchcraft, occult practices, or New Age practices, a demonstration of power through the Holy Spirit is often necessary for evangelism of these groups as they fully understand the power of the spiritual realm, at times, even more so than some Christians.

GLOBAL RESEARCH ON DEMONS AND EXORCISMS

In the modern, American worldview, many people struggle to accept a spiritual worldview that is foundational to accepting that a person can be influenced by a demon. Instead, these people, even many Christians, choose to deny this worldview, and thus, demons are irrelevant to them or treated as nonexistent. While I do not believe that "there is a demon behind every corner," I do believe that this mindset has caused an ignorance to the spiritual reality that we live in today. Regardless, denial does not negate the effects of demonic powers in the world. To look at this from a global perspective provides further understanding as most cultures around the world openly embrace a spiritual worldview. Interestingly, many of these cultures are not Christian but still have a greater understanding of the spirit world and an acceptance of it than most Americans.

EXPERIENCES FROM HAITI

From our work in many nations, especially Haiti, the spirit world is as real as the natural world. Voodoo is not a hidden practice but is very open and obvious. This reality impacts how many Haitians live and function on a daily basis. One trend that always broke my heart was watching many Haitian families place offerings of food on demonic altars in order to appease their ancestors and attempt to prevent demonic torment. In most cases, these families would literally be barely surviving day to day and starving at times, yet they continued to religiously place their food offerings on these altars to other gods. The freedom and power they found when they came to Christ also came with a great blessing as they no longer had to offer sacrifices on those altars to demons.

Another example from Haiti was the willingness to receive a blessing, regardless of the source that it came through. Many Haitians willingly accepted the "blessings" of a voodoo priest as good, even many Christians. They did not discern the evil that was in operation behind these "blessings." As a result, they often received some form of a curse attached to the blessing. However, the power of Christ was still greater than these curses in any and every form. Let's briefly evaluate how much of the world outside America views the spiritual world and its cultural impacts.

GLOBAL RESEARCH

After extensive global research, in 1987, Marcus J. Borg identified several typical traits that are associated with someone who is considered demonized: "self-destructive behavior, sweating, seizures, convulsions, and unexplainable knowledge."[197] Another interesting discovery was made by Stevan L. Davies in 1995. Through cross-cultural, anthropological studies, he came to the conclusion that demonization can "be interpreted as a form of multiple personality disorder."[198] In 2012, Amanda Witmer came to the conclusion that demonization "is a widespread phenomenon, virtually universal in human experience."[199] Paul Rhodes Eddy and Gregory Boyd discovered a similar but further defined list as Borg in 2007 through their global research of common characteristics of a demonized person in other cultures:

> Uncontrollable and uncharacteristic outbursts of violent behavior, sometimes exhibiting strength seemingly beyond their natural capacities; a temporary ability to speak in languages they did not learn; manifest bizarre physical behavior that seems to go beyond anyone's natural capacities—for example, fantastic facial contortions and physically improbable limb rotations.[200]

Both the lists of Borg and of Eddy and Boyd reflect the descriptions of demonization found within the New Testament.[201]

Another valuable insight comes from Stephen Pattemore, a missionary and Bible translator who works specifically among animistic tribes in Thailand. From his experiences and research within this culture, he states that a common observation emerges. Demons and evil spirits have a chief spirit who is often the source of sickness and is viewed as in control of the earthly world.[202] This furthers the demonic hierarchy that has clearly been discussed throughout this book.

EFFECTS ON THEOLOGY

Another valuable discovery of Eddy and Boyd within this discussion is the impact of modern Western culture on theological scholarship, especially those who translate scripture. They came to the conclusion that because many academics and scholars attempt to study through the lens of objectivity, they ultimately deny human experience in their research. Therefore, they "reject supernatural elements as a part of the natural world."[203] This means that contemporary scholarship and even biblical translation can be impacted by a strictly natural worldview that denies any form of supernatural experiences. The experiences of anything spiritual are ultimately rejected with this practice because they cannot be proven by science or logic.

Oftentimes, scholars dismiss the supernatural aspects of scripture as "hearsay, legend, hallucination, psychosomatic hysteria, exaggeration, intentional fabrication, or something of the sort."[204] This would explain why many biblical translations change the language of scripture to fit a modern Western worldview devoid of the supernatural world. As proven previously in this book, there are many occurrences of specific, demonic entities being changed from their proper names to natural animals or elements of nature.[205] Further, Eddy and Boyd's research reveals a need for Western scholars to take a more global perspective in scholarship which would reveal a supernatural worldview that aligns more with the scriptures than with the Western worldview of science, rationalism, and logic.

Another term that is helpful in this discussion is the concept of demons and demonic spirits as being "demythologized." Some scholars use this term to identify where some biblical translators "came to deny the existence of all other divine beings besides Yahweh."[206] This would account for many of the proper names of spiritual deities that have been translated as natural beings or dismissed completely.

Dr. Michael Heiser further states, "Another perspective of 'de-mythologizing' is to acknowledge that biblical writers stripped foreign deities of autonomy or independent personality without denying their existence."[207] He states that in scripture, this is the case for the god of death, Mot, which is described previously in detail in Chapter 5. In *The Dictionary of Deities and Demons in the Bible*, the editors share this same view as Heiser and commonly attribute this as the reason why many of these named entities are not accurately translated in most scriptures.[208]

AFRICAN STUDIES

In 2019, by extensively studying modern African cultures, Marius Nel made an interesting discovery in which he concluded that "African traditional religion is analogous to the worldview of early Christians"[209] meaning they are essentially the same. His position is, "For Africans, what happens on earth is directly interrelated with what happens in the dimension of the spiritual, agreeing with the cosmic principalities and powers that provide the mystical causality of a worldview found in the New Testament."[210] After working in Haiti for over a decade, this aligns with the cultural beliefs we encountered there which were rooted deeply in the spiritual realm, even more than the natural realm in some cases. Scholar Craig Keener came to this conclusion concerning demonization through a global, cultural understanding: "Beliefs in control by a foreign spirit are so common among unrelated cultures that they appear to reflect a common human experience of some sort more than a mere custom."[211]

DEMONS AND SICKNESS

As mentioned previously, there is a strong correlation in scripture between casting out demons and healing the sick. In the Western worldview, with its emphasis on mental health and modern medicinal practices, it would be extremely rare for any form of sickness or disease to be diagnosed as caused by a demonic source; that would mean that exorcism would be the cure, not medication or treatment. However, this is abnormal when compared with the rest of the world and most other cultures. To simplify, global research shows that demonization can often explain a person's illnesses, especially in the mental health field.[212] In fact, medical anthropologist, George Murdock, states that over 97 percent of the global societies he has studied associate demonization with illness.[213] From his studies specifically in India, Frederick Smith came to the conclusion that demonization is "a central concept in the realm of mental health."[214]

In 2022, the National Institute of Mental Health (NIMH) stated that 23.1 percent of American adults struggle with mental illness which equates to 59.3 million people.[215] An honest evaluation of the need for deliverance ministry must be evaluated with these alarming statistics. I am not saying that every form or case of mental illness is caused by a demon; however, I would argue that through a global perspective and a spiritual worldview, some of these cases quite possibly could be. As with the case of any illness, whether it be physical, mental, or spiritual, Jesus is the answer: "*That evening they brought to him many who were possessed by demons, and he cast out the spirits with a word and cured all who were sick*" (Matthew 8:16 NRSV). We have frequently witnessed the power of Jesus to deliver people from various forms of sickness. The testimonies of freedom from depression, anxiety, and fear are quite common and life-changing for the individual.

CHAPTER 13

SUMMARY AND NEXT STEPS

We began this journey by sharing with you our life experiences gathered over 26 years of walking with Jesus. In the beginning, we could never have imagined stepping into such a high level of deliverance ministry and carrying this message to the nations as we are now. As you have read through these pages, perhaps you have gained clarity or realized how complex deliverance can be. It is far more than simply declaring, "Come out in the name of Jesus." Regardless of where you are in this journey, we hope you find encouragement in the testimony that I shared at the beginning, when the demons laughed at me in a restaurant parking lot many years ago. Today, demons may begin with laughter when they initially manifest, but they almost always end with cries of agony at their departure, once all of their curses are broken.

We have explored one of the foundational principles of Jesus's ministry: His confrontation with the powers of darkness in Caesarea Philippi where He declared the birth of His church. Just as He sent His followers into the dark territories of the earth with the promise that the gates of Hades would not prevail, He continues to call us today to confront darkness in the earth and set people free. Our hope is that this book will inspire local churches to reevaluate how they bring people into fellowship and covenant with Jesus. Specifically, we pray for a renewed understanding of the practice of baptism—a gateway moment when demons are severed from individuals, thus ushering them into new life in Christ.

While we celebrate all who love God and serve His people by bringing freedom, this book outlines what we call *Bloodline Deliverance*, emphasizing four key principles:

- The revelation of different categories and kinds of demons.
- How demons work in conjunction with high-ranking territorial principalities.
- The vital connection between deliverance from demons and the breaking of curses.
- The effective use of a brief, demonic interrogation to expose and dismantle strongholds.

It is essential for local churches, under the guidance of their shepherds and elders, to take up the responsibility of deliverance for the people that God has entrusted to them. While special services and guest ministers can bring invaluable impartation and momentum, the ongoing work of deliverance must be a part of the local church's ministry.

If you feel called to go deeper into the ministry of deliverance, I invite you to explore my One-Year Deliverance Mentoring Community. You can find more information about this and other resources at my website: MikeBrewer.life.

ENDNOTES

1 This principle comes from Luke 10:1–11.

2 Cf. Acts 19:13–17.

3 Cf. Gal. 5:6; 1 Cor. 13:1–3.

4 Michael S. Heiser, *Reversing Hermon: Enoch, the Watchers, and the Forgotten Mission of Jesus Christ*, kindle ed., (Crane, MO: Defender, 2017), loc 1668.

5 Cf. 1 Kings 12.

6 Cf. Jos 11:17; Judges 3:3.

7 Heiser, *Hermon*, loc 1666.

8 Cf. Matt. 10:1.

9 Gustaf Aulén, *Christus Victor*, (Austin, TX: Wise Path, 2016), 89.

10 *The Apostolic Tradition*, attributed to Hippolytus of Rome, 3rd century. English translation from *On the Apostolic Tradition*, edited and translated by Alistair Stewart-Sykes, St. Vladimir's Seminary Press, 2001.

11 Catechetical Lectures, Lecture 19: On the Mysteries II: Baptism, circa 4th century. English translation from *Nicene and Post-Nicene Fathers*, Series 2, Vol. 7, edited by Philip Schaff, Hendrickson Publishers, 1994.

12 *Traditio Apostolica*, attributed to Hippolytus of Rome, 3rd century. English translation from *The Apostolic Tradition of Hippolytus*, translated by Burton Scott Easton, Cambridge University Press, 1934.

13 Michael S. Heiser, *I Dare You Not to Bore Me with the Bible*, kindle ed., (Bellingham, WA: Lexham Press. 2014), loc. 132.

14 G. R. Knight, *Philosophy and Education: An Introduction in Christian Perspective*. 4th ed., (Berrien Springs, MI: Andrews University Press, 1998), 17.

15 "New Research Explores Teenage Views and Behavior Regarding the Supernatural," Barna Group, January 23, 2006, Accessed May 9, 2023. *https://www.barna.com/research/new-research-explores-teenage-views-and-behavior-regarding-the-supernatural/*.

16 "Beetlejuice Beetlejuice," *https://www.imdb.com/title/tt2049403/*, Accessed December 6, 2024.

17 "Hocus Pocus," *https://www.boxofficemojo.com/releasegroup/gr2492682757/*, Accessed on December 6, 2024.

18 "Hocus Pocus," *https://www.imdb.com/title/tt0107120/*, Accessed on December 6, 2024.

19 "Review Wicked," *https://www.americamagazine.org/arts-culture/2024/11/22/wicked-film-musical-catholic-249324*, Accessed on December 6, 2024.

20 Michael S. Heiser, *The Unseen Realm: Recovering the Supernatural Worldview of the Bible*, (Bellingham, WA: Lexham, 2015), 29.

21 Cf. 1 Kings 22:19-22; John 4:24; Heb. 1:14.

22 Michael S. Hesier, *Demons: What the Bible Really Says about the Powers of Darkness*, (Bellingham, WA: Lexham, 2020), 6.

23 Heiser, *Demons*, 7.

24 Clinton E. Arnold, *3 Crucial Questions about Spiritual Warfare*, kindle ed., (Grand Rapids, MI: Baker, 1997), loc. 2889.

25 Michael S. Heiser, "Deuteronomy 32:8 and the Sons of God," *Bibliotheca Sacra*, vol. 158, (January-March 2001), 61.

26 Cf. Deut. 29:26; 32:16; Judges 2:11-12; 10:6; 1 Kings 11:4-10; 12:28-30; 2 Kings 17:11; 1 Chron. 5:25; 2 Chron. 25:14-15; 28:23; Jer. 32:35.

27 Heiser, *Demons*, 218.

28 Arnold, *Questions*, loc. 2927.

29 Arnold, *Questions*, loc. 2917.

30 Arnold, *Questions*, loc. 2910.

31 Arnold, *Questions*, loc. 2948.

32 Cf. Lev. 17:7; Deut. 32:17; Ps. 106:37.

33 Heiser, "Deuteronomy," 54.

34 Heiser, *Unseen*, 38.

35 Heiser, *Unseen*, 38.

36 Cf. Ps. 1:5; 37:32-33; 109; 94:21.

37 Cf. Is 1:7; 5:23, 28; 10:1-2; Jer. 22:3; Amos 3:6-7; 5:7, 12; Zeph. 3:3; Zech. 7:9-10.

38 Julian Morgenstern, "The Mythological Background of Psalm 82," *Hebrew Union College Annual*, vol. 14, (1939) 31.

39 Morgenstern, "Psalm 82," 33.

40 Tremper III. Longman and David E. Garland, eds., *The Expositor's Bible Commentary: Psalms*, vol. 5 (Grand Rapids, MI: Zondervan Pub. House, 2008), 293.

41 Heiser, "Deuteronomy," 53.

42 Heiser, *Unseen*, 130.

43 Heiser, "Deuteronomy," 53.

44 Heiser, *Unseen*, 130.

45 Hart, *Truth*, 128.

46 F.F. Bruce, Gordon D. Fee, Joel B. Green, and Neb B. Stonehouse, eds., *The Letter to the Colossians, The New International Commentary on the New Testament,* (Grand Rapids, MI: William B. Eerdmans, 2018), 238.

47 G.B. Caird, *New Testament Theology*, revised ed., (New York, NY: Oxford University, 1994), 102.

48 Cf. Rom. 8:38; 1 Cor. 10:20; Eph. 1:21; 2:2; 3:10; 6:12; Col. 1:16; 2:15.

49 Ronn A. Johnson, "The Old Testament Background for Paul's Use of Powers and Principalities," PhD diss., (Dallas Theological Seminary, 2004), 7.

50 Johnson, "Background," 7.

51 See Acts 22:1-5.

52 Johnson, "Background," 14.

53 Cf. Eph. 6:12; Col. 2:15; 1 Cor. 15:24; Eph. 3:10.

54 F.F. Bruce, *The Epistles to the Colossians, to Philemon, and to the Ephesians*, New International Commentary on the New Testament (Grand Rapids, MI: William B. Eerdmans, 1984), *ProQuest Ebook, http://ebookcentral.proquest.com/lib/dtl/detail.action?docID=4860132*, 446.

55 Dr. Harold R. Eberle, *Systematic Theology for the New Apostolic Reformation: An Exposition in Father-Son Theology*, 2nd ed., (Yakima, WA: Worldcast, 2016), 85.

56 Eberle, *Systematic*, 86.

57 Heiser, *I Dare You*, loc 145.

58 Cf. Job 26:10.

59 Heiser, *I Dare You*, loc 145.

60 Cf. Gen. 7:11; 8:2; Ps. 78:23; 33:7.

61 "Epouranios," Strong's G2032, *https://www.blueletterbible.org/lexicon/g2032/nasb95/mgnt/0-1*, Accessed December 5, 2024.

62 Cf. Eph. 1:3, 20; 2:6; 3:10; 6:12; Heb. 3:1; 6:4; 8:5; 9:23; 11:16; 12:22.

63 Cf. Gen. 1:9-10.

64 Cf. 2 Pet. 3:5.

65 Cf. 1 Sam. 2:8; Job 38:4-6; Ps. 104:5.

66 Cf. Prov. 9:18; Ps. 6:4-5; 18:4-5.

67 Heiser, *Demons*, loc 680.

68 Heiser, *I Dare You*, loc 158.

69 Cf. Jonah 2:5-6.

70 "milkōṯ," Strong's H4446, *https://www.blueletterbible.org/lexicon/h4446/nasb20/wlc/0-1/*, Accessed December 5, 2024.

71 "malkâ," Strong's H4436, *https://www.blueletterbible.org/lexicon/h4436/nasb20/wlc/0-1/*, Accessed December 5, 2024.

72 Rebecca Greenwood, *Dethroning the Queen of Heaven: Cancel This Demon's Ancient Agenda to Destroy Your Life and Control Nations*, (Shippensburg, PA: Destiny Image, 2024), 17.

73 Ibid.

74 Greenwood, *Dethroning*, 16.

75 "Asherah," In *The Dictionary of Deities and Demons in the Bible*, Edited by Karel Van Der Toorn, Bob Becking, and Peter W. Van Der Horst, 2nd ed., (Grand Rapids, MI: William B. Eerdmans, 1999), 102.

76 "Asherah," *Dictionary*, 104.

77 "Asherah," *Dictionary*, 99.

78 Ibid.

79 Greenwood, *Dethroning*, 161-162.

80 Heiser, *Demons*, 177.

81 "Baal," In *The Dictionary of Deities and Demons in the Bible*, Edited by Karel Van Der Toorn, Bob Becking, and Peter W. Van Der Horst, 2nd ed., (Grand Rapids, MI: William B. Eerdmans, 1999), 132.

82 Heiser, *Demons*, 14.

83 Greenwood, *Dethroning*, 160.

84 Cf. 1 Kings 16:30-33.

85 Greenwood, *Dethroning*, 159.

86 Cf. 1 Kings 18:4.

87 "Marduk," In *The Dictionary of Deities and Demons in the Bible*, Edited by Karel Van Der Toorn, Bob Becking, and Peter W. Van Der Horst, 2nd ed., (Grand Rapids, MI: William B. Eerdmans, 1999), 544.

88 Ibid.

89 "mᵊrōḏaḵ," Strong's H4781, *https://www.blueletterbible.org/lexicon/h4781/nasb20/wlc/0-1/*, Accessed December 11, 2024.

90 "Marduk," *Dictionary*, 548.

91 "Constellations," In *The Dictionary of Deities and Demons in the Bible*, Edited by Karel Van Der Toorn, Bob Becking, and Peter W. Van Der Horst, 2nd ed., (Grand Rapids, MI: William B. Eerdmans, 1999), 202.

92 "mōleḵ," Strong's H4432, *https://www.blueletterbible.org/lexicon/h4432/nasb20/wlc/0-1/*, Accessed December 11, 2024.

93 "Constellations, *Dictionary*, 202.

94 Ibid.

95 "Divination, Magic," In *The IVP Bible Dictionary Series: Dictionary of the Old Testament Prophets*, Edited by Dr. Mark J. Boda and J. Gordon McConville, (Downers Grove, IL: InterVarsity Press, 2012), 385.

96 "Divination," *Dictionary*, 384.

97 "Divination," *Dictionary*, 385.

98 "Divination," *Dictionary*, 386.

99 Joy L. Vaughn, *Phenomenal Phenomena: Biblical and Multicultural Accounts of Spirits and Exorcism*, (Waco, TX: Baylor, 2023), 3.

100 "Divination," *Dictionary*, 385.

101 "magos," Strong's G3097, *https://www.blueletterbible.org/lexicon/g3097/nasb20/mgnt/0-1/*, Accessed on December 11, 2024.

102 "sikûṯ," Strong's H5522, *https://www.blueletterbible.org/lexicon/h5522/nasb20/wlc/0-1/*, Accessed on December 11, 2024.

103 "kîyûn," Strong's H3594, *https://www.blueletterbible.org/lexicon/h3594/nasb20/wlc/0-1/*, Accessed on December 11, 2024.

104 "Kaiwan," In *The Dictionary of Deities and Demons in the Bible*, Edited by Karel Van Der Toorn, Bob Becking, and Peter W. Van Der Horst, 2nd ed., (Grand Rapids, MI: William B. Eerdmans, 1999), 478.

105 Ibid.

106 F.F. Bruce, *The Book of the Acts, The New International Commentary on the New Testament* (Grand Rapids, MI: Wm. B. Eerdmans Publishing Co., 1988), 144.

107 Bruce, *Acts*, 145.

108 Bruce, *Acts*, 145.

109 "The Divine Guardians of the Imperial Family in Japanese Mythology," *https://japanese.mythologyworldwide.com/the-divine-guardians-of-the-imperial-family/*, Published on October 16, 2024, Accessed on December 12, 2024.

110 Heiser, *Demons*, loc 586.

111 Heiser, *Demons*, loc 636.

112 Heiser, *Demons*, loc 615.

113 Heiser, *Unseen*, loc 3155.

114 Heisier, *Unseen*, loc 3165.

115 Heiser, *Unseen*, loc 3169.

116 Cf. Is 34:14.

117 K. Schifferdecker, "Creation Theology," In *The IVP Bible Dictionary Series: Dictionary of the Old Testament: Wisdom, Poetry, Writings*, Edited by Tremper Longman III and Peter Enns, (Downers Grove, IL: InterVarsity Press, 2008), 212.

118 "The Story of Lotus Flower and The 4 Types of Lotus in Buddhism," *https://bstcthanka.com/blogs/mandala/the-story-of-lotus-flower-significance-hidden-buddhist-story*, Published on July 31, 2023, Accessed on December 9, 2024.

119 "Lakshmi: Goddess of Prosperity," *https://www.hinduamerican.org/blog/lakshmi,* Published on December 6, 2017, Accessed on December 9, 2024.

120 "Belial," In *The Dictionary of Deities and Demons in the Bible*, Edited by Karel Van Der Toorn, Bob Becking, and Peter W. Van Der Horst, 2nd ed., (Grand Rapids, MI: William B. Eerdmans, 1999), 169.

121 Bill T. Arnold, *1 and 2 Samuel, The NIV Application Commentary,* (Grand Rapids, MI: Zondervan, 2003), 94.

122 Heiser, *Hermon*, loc 1668.

123 Heiser, *Hermon*, loc 1666.

124 Cf. 1 Kings 12.

125 Cf. Jos 11:17; Judges 3:3.

126 Heiser, *Hermon*, loc 1674.

127 Heiser, *Hermon*, loc 1674.

128 Heiser, *Hermon*, loc 1683.

129 "Gates," In *The IVP Bible Dictionary Series: Dictionary of Biblical Imagery*, Edited by Leland Ryken, James C. Wilhoit, and Tremper Longman III, (Downers Grove, IL: InterVarsity Press, 1998), 321.

130 Cf. Jer. 49:31.

131 Cf. Is 28:6.

132 Heiser, *Hermon*, loc 1674.

133 "Mot," In *The Dictionary of Deities and Demons in the Bible*, Edited by Karel Van Der Toorn, Bob Becking, and Peter W. Van Der Horst, 2nd ed., (Grand Rapids, MI: William B. Eerdmans, 1999), 598.

134 "Mot," *Dictionary*, 599.

135 Cf. 1 Chron. 22:8; 28:3.

136 Cf. 1 Sam. 17:34-37.

137 Cf. 1 Sam. 17:48-51.

138 "Belial," *Dictionary*, 169.

139 Heiser, *Demons, 30.*

140 "Mot," *Dictionary*, 601.

141 "Molech," In *The Dictionary of Deities and Demons in the Bible*, Edited by Karel Van Der Toorn, Bob Becking, and Peter W. Van Der Horst, 2nd ed., (Grand Rapids, MI: William B. Eerdmans, 1999), 581.

142 "Mot," *Dictionary*, 601.

143 Ibid.

144 "genos," Strong's G1085, *https://www.blueletterbible.org/lexicon/g1085/nasb20/mgnt/0-1/*, Accessed on December 3, 2024.

145 Mark Cartwright, "Templo Mayor," *https://www.worldhistory.org/Templo_Mayor/*, Published on February 5, 2016, Accessed on December 5, 2024.

146 Ibid.

147 Rebecca Greenwood, *Authority to Tread: A Practical Guide for Strategic-Level Spiritual Warfare*, (Grand Rapids, MI: Chosen, 2005), 26-28.

148 Cf. Eph. 4:11-13.

149 Mike Brewer, *The Self Deliverance Guide: Your Step-by-Step Process to Freedom from Bondage and Closing of Spiritual Doors*, (Mike Brewer, 2021), 22.

150 Arnold, *Questions*, loc. 2770.

151 Heiser, *Demons*, 261.

152 C.E. Arnold, "Ephesus," In *The IVP Bible Dictionary Series: Dictionary of Paul and His Letters*, Edited by Gerald F. Hawthorne, Ralph P. Martin, Daniel G. Reid, (Downers Grove, IL: InterVarsity Press, 1995), n.p.

153 L.M. McDonald, "Ephesus," In *The IVP Bible Dictionary Series: Dictionary of New Testament Background*, Edited by Craig A. Evans and Stanley E. Porter, (Downers Grove, IL: InterVarsity Press, 2000), n.p.

154 Darrell Bock, *Ephesians, Tyndale New Testament Commentary Series,* vol. 10, (Downers Grove, IL: InterVarsity Press, 2019), 197.

155 Cf. Rom. 13:12; 2 Cor. 6:7; 10:3–6; 1 Thess. 5:8; 1 Tim. 1:18; 2 Tim. 2:3–4.

156 Bock, *Ephesians*, 198.

157 "Armor," In *The IVP Bible Dictionary Series: Dictionary of Biblical Imagery*, Edited by Leland Ryken, James C. Wilhoit, and Tremper Longman III (Downers Grove, IL: InterVarsity Press, 1998), 44.

158 Benjamin L. Merkle, *Ephesians, Exegetical Guide to the Greek New Testament* (Nashville, TN: BandH Publishing, 2016), 211.

159 Bruce, *Colossians*, 244.

160 See Eph. 2:1–7.

161 Clinton E. Arnold, Frank S. Thielman, and Steven M. Baugh. *Ephesians, Philippians, Colossians, Philemon, Zondervan Illustrated Bible Backgrounds Commentary* (Grand Rapids, MI: Zondervan, 2015), 82.

162 Merkle, *Ephesians*, 213.

163 See Luke 11:21-22.

164 "Armor," In *The IVP Bible Dictionary Series: Dictionary of Biblical Imagery*, Edited by Leland Ryken, James C. Wilhoit, and Tremper Longman III (Downers Grove, IL: InterVarsity Press, 1998), 44.

165 Cf. John 10:10.

166 Bock, *Ephesians*, 199.

167 Cf. Rom. 12:2; Eph. 4:23; 2 Cor. 10:5.

168 "Possession," *https://www.merriam-webster.com/dictionary/possession*, Accessed on December 5, 2024.

169 Darrell L. Bock, *Luke, The NIV Application Commentary*, (Grand Rapids, MI: Zondervan, 1996), 127.

170 *Luke-Acts, The Expositor's Bible Commentary*, Edited by Tremper Longman, III and David Garland, vol. 10, kindle ed., (Grand Rapids, MI: Zondervan, 2007), location 3620.

171 Heiser, *Demons*, loc 586.

172 Cf. Matt. 4:24; Mark 1:23-26; Luke 4:33-35; 41.

173 E.P. Sanders, *The Historical Figure of Jesus* (London, England: Penguin, 1993), 149.

174 Donald Alfred Hagner, *Matthew 1-13, Word Biblical Commentary,* vol. 33A, (Grand Rapids, MI: Zondervan, 1993), 79.

175 "synechō," Strong's G4912, *https://www.blueletterbible.org/lexicon/g4912/nasb95/mgnt/0-1/,* Accessed on December 10, 2024.

176 Hagner, *Matthew*, 80.

177 Hagner, *Matthew*, 80.

178 Sanders, *Historical*,149.

179 Cf. Matt. 8:16; 28-34; 9:32-34; 12:22-24; 15:22-28; 17:14-18; Mark 1:32-34; Luke 4:40-41; 6:17-19; 8:2; 11:14.

180 "ekballō," Strong's G1544, *https://www.blueletterbible.org/lexicon/g1544/nasb95/mgnt/0-1/*, Accessed on December 9, 2024.

181 Jeff Oliver, *Pentecost to the Present: The Holy Spirit's Enduring Work in the Church, Book One: Early Prophetic and Spiritual Gifts Movements*, (Newberry, FL: Bridge-Logos, 2017), 9.

182 Oliver, *Pentecost*, 49.

183 Oliver, *Pentecost*, 50.

184 Justin Martyr, *The Second Apology of Justin*, Alexander Roberts, The Ante-Nicene Christian Library: Translations of the Writings of the Father down to A.D. 325, (1867), 1:189.

185 Origen, *Against Celsus*, ANCL 4:473: CC 19.

186 Oliver, *Pentecost*, 77.

187 NPNF, 2nd Series, vol.2; *Socrates Scholasticus, Ecclesiastical History*, Bk.4, Chap.27:MM 32.

188 Oliver, *Pentecost*, 77.

189 NPNF, vol.8, *The Book of St. Basil on the Spirit*, chap.29, sect.74: MM 32.

190 St. Athanasius, *The Life of Antony*, 89.

191 Athanasius, *Antony*, 89.

192 Oliver, *Pentecost*, 123.

193 Oliver, *Pentecost*, 124.

194 Rufinus, *Historia Monachorum in Aegypto*, MM 86–89.

195 John Calvin, "Institutes of the Christian Religion Book IV" F.L. Cross, ed. (1515) *Institutes of the Christian Religion*, Book IV (New York: Oxford, 1982): "Pope Gregory I," Wikipedia: en.wikipedia.org/wiki/Pope_Gregory_I (Accessed 15 November 2012).

196 Oliver, *Pentecost*, 153.

197 Marcus J. Borg, *A New Vision: Spirit, Culture, and the Life of Discipleship* (San Francisco: Harper and Row, 1987), 62.

198 Stevan L. Davies, *Jesus the Healer: Possession, Trance, and the Origins of Christianity* (New York: Continuum, 1995), 89.

199 Amanda Witmer, *Jesus the Galilean Exorcist: His Exorcisms in Social and Political Context* (London: TandT Clark, 2012), 24.

200 Paul Rhodes Eddy and Gregory A. Boyd, *The Jesus Legend: A Case fo the Historical Reliability of the Synoptic Jesus Tradition* (Grand Rapids: Baker, 2007).

201 Cf. Matt. 4:24; 8:16, 28; 9:32; 12:22; 15:22-24; 17:14-18; Mark 1:34; 5:15; 6:13; Luke 4:33-41; 8:26-36; 9:37-42; 11:14; Acts 8:7; 10:38; 16:16-19; 19:12,16.

202 Stephen Pattemore, "Principalities and Powers in Urak Lawói," from the journal, *The Bible Translator* 45, no. 1 (January 1994), *https://journals-sagepub-com.dtl.idm.oclc.org/doi/10.1177/026009359404500302.*

203 Eddy and Boyd, *Jesus*, 67.

204 Eddy and Boyd, *Jesus*, 69.

205 See previous section in chapter 3, What Are Demons?

206 Heiser, *Demons*, 268.

207 Ibid.

208 "Mot," *Dictionary*, 600.

209 Marius Nel, "The African Background of Pentecostal Theology: A Critical Perspective," *In die Skriflig* 53.4 (2019): 1–8.

210 Nel, "African," 1.

211 Craig Keener, "Spirit Possession as a Cross-cultural Experience," BBR 20.2 (2010): 217.

212 Vaughn, *Phenomena*, 80.

213 George Murdock, *Theories of Illness: A World Survey*, (Pittsburg, PA: University of Pittsburgh, 1980), 72.

214 Frederick M. Smith, "Possession, Embodiment, and Ritual in Mental Health Care in India," *Journal of Ritual Studies* 24.2 (2010): 22.

215 "Mental Illness," *https://www.nimh.nih.gov/health/statistics/mental-illness*, Updated September 2024, Accessed on december 8, 2024.

ABOUT MIKE AND ANDREA BREWER

Mike and Andrea Brewer are seasoned missionaries, intercessors, and apostolic pioneers, dedicated to advancing the supernatural Kingdom of God. Founders of The Well Global Alliance, they have served in Haiti, India, and Cambodia, catalyzing two church planting movements now numbering thousands of churches. Partnering strategically with Kingdom leaders, they assemble fivefold teams to break open regions. At the core of their work is a commitment to modeling, equipping, mentoring, and sending forth warriors to fulfill their God-given destinies.

In the Right Hands, This Book Will Change Lives!

Most of the people who need this message will not be looking for this book. To change their lives, you need to **put a copy of this book in their hands.**

Our ministry is constantly seeking methods to find the people who need this anointed message to change their lives. **Will you help us reach these people?**

Extend this ministry by sowing three, five, ten, or *even more* books today and change people's lives for the better! Your generosity will be part of catalyzing the Great Awakening that many have been prophesying and praying for.